THE

INVESTIGATOR'S

HANDBOOK

This book is intended as a guide to private investigation. The author and publisher expressly do not advocate any activity that could be illegal in any manner. The reader is advised to consult with his or her attorney concerning applicable federal and state laws. The author and publisher assume no responsibility for any injury and/or damage to persons or property which is incurred as a consequence, directly or indirectly, of the use and application of any of the contents of this work.

THIS IS A CARLTON BOOK

Carlton Books Limited
20 Mortimer Street
London
W1T 3JW

This edition published 2001

10 9 8 7 6 5 4 3 2 1

Text and design copyright © 2001 Carlton Books Limited

A CIP catalogue record for this book is available from the British Library

ISBN Hardback 1 84222 500 6
ISBN Paperback 1 84222 376 3

Project Editor: Luke Friend
Design: Vaseem Bhatti
Production: Lisa French

Printed in Great Britain

THE
PRIVATE
INVESTIGATOR'S
HANDBOOK

DR K GAVIN

CARLTON
BOOKS

Contents

List of Illustrations

INTRODUCTION

Anyone who has ever sought to uncover the disappearance of a long-lost heirloom, or endeavoured to follow a friend's mischievous partner, can loosely be called a 'private investigator'. The term 'private investigator' (PI), or 'detective', conveys an air of mystery and romanticism to the uninitiated, and appears to be the sort of job that is carried out by faceless characters clad in dirty raincoats, skulking in dimly lit corners of shady hotel rooms and rain-drenched back-streets.

Many see the PI as a civilian spy, a one-man band trying to make a meagre living from day-to-day routine enquiries waiting in anticipation of the 'big job'.

So what exactly is a private investigator? The ex-police officer serving papers from the court in divorce proceedings? The retired person whose sense of curiosity and justice stirs them into action? Or the slick, quick, industrial-espionage specialist who continually tries to foil and outwit unscrupulous business people who are bent on financial and political power?

Well, there are those who fit all of these descriptions and many more, but the term private investigator is in fact an umbrella under which many diverse bodies take shelter.

The type of work carried out by investigators is as diverse as the people who take up the profession. As well as the usual, widely accepted and well-known matrimonial and divorce work, the modern PI can be called upon to act as a professional witness, which involves him in gathering evidence to support legal applications put before a court – often in disputes between neighbours. Sometimes the PI will be called upon to work in criminal investigations to help prove a theft or some other crime, and to gather evidence to be given to the police or as part of a court case being presented before a judge. On the other hand, the PI may have to work for the defence of a suspected criminal, meticulously sifting through the evidence and challenging any inconsistencies or locating and interviewing possible defence witnesses.

A PI will also be expected to carry out investigations to locate and prove that a firm or individual is manufacturing or supplying goods or products without the license-holder's consent. Retail and manufacturing companies will often call upon the services of a PI to work undercover or carry out covert surveillance, gathering information to determine how their employees operate out of sight of management, or to identify individuals or teams who are involved in theft, or using equipment for their own benefit. When firms are in dispute with their employees, or when they suspect a breach of employment or a director's contract, a PI will be expected to gather and collate evidence to prove any breaches.

Insurance companies will call upon a PI to take statements from claimants, and carry out surveillance using video filming to show that a claimant – although saying that he/she is unable to work – is in fact fit and healthy. Another insurance application is the investigation of accidents, which usually includes detailed drawings and high-quality photography to support witness statements. Tracing missing persons can also account for a great deal of the investigator's day-to-day work.

A PI will often be called upon to carry out status and credit reports on individuals and companies. In the preparation of these reports, the PI will have to carry out extensive data checks to ascertain what assets or debts the suspect has. Data checks are not the only means of identifying a person's financial status. On occasions the true picture will only unfold after a PI has carried out physical checks at locations used by the suspect, no matter where those locations are in the world.

One aspect of a PI's life that is often overlooked is repossessions. This can involve repossessing buildings, equipment and vehicles – usually for hire companies, credit and loan companies or mortgage holders and landlords. This type of work may begin by the PI having to carry out trace enquiries to locate the exact whereabouts of the vehicle or equipment concerned. Once it has been found, the PI will then be expected to take possession and have the items returned to their owners. Taking possession of a person's home or business premises is an area of work that can be extremely emotionally charged. In these circumstances, a PI will be expected to keep calm and carry on with the job in a very professional way – even when everyone around him is venting their anger and frustration. Stalking and harassment cases also require a great deal of investigative skill and understanding; PIs are extensively used in gathering evidence to support legal action against the perpetrators of these crimes.

What can certainly be said about the life of a PI is that the work will always be varied and often demanding. Should you decide to join the PI's world of espionage and intrigue, you can be guaranteed that the work will stretch your intellect and your endurance to their limits. As a PI you will have to be able to go from extreme to extreme. You will often be sitting at your desk working on everyday mundane tasks, such as report writing or writing up your files, when the telephone will ring and you will be launched into an investigation that will involve you having to work at full stretch in unfamiliar surroundings or dressed in camouflage clothing, operating still and video cameras as you spy on an unsuspecting criminal. Lord Robert Baden-Powell's Scout Movement uses the motto 'Be Prepared' – an approach that all PIs should adopt. It's believed that Lord Baden-Powell first used this term when he was working as a spy in the British military.

Being prepared is not just about thinking: it is also about proper preparation. Much of the equipment used by today's PIs is straight from the spying game, and requires a considerable amount of training and constant usage before it can be operated in a thoroughly professional way. Ongoing training will have to be undertaken to maintain the high standard that a client expects from their investigator. Equipment is a very important aspect of a PI's work, and could include: specially adapted vehicles that are fitted with periscopes, video recorders and sound equipment; micro transmitters and miniature audio recording systems; and tracking devices, which can easily be fixed to a vehicle and then emit a signal so that the tailing PI can follow the occupant to a secret rendezvous. All of these, and many more spy gadgets – coupled with the private investigator's cunning and ingenuity – bring justice and peace of mind to thousands of clients every day.

The purpose of this book is to acquaint you, the initiate, with the secret work of the PI and with the techniques and equipment used in the business of covert observations of persons, places, objects and the gathering of evidence to show civil, criminal, anti-social and unsociable acts. Although the law relating to private investigators and the methods and equipment they use change from country to country, the techniques and basic expertise are the same the world over.

Perhaps the best known of all private detectives was Sir Arthur Conan Doyle's character Sherlock Holmes, whose legendary exploits give us a sense of professionalism that tugs at the establishment's belief that the only true investigators are those who are trained and employed by the establishment. Over recent years, there has been a wide acceptance that the authorities do not necessarily hold the key to professional investigation. As a result the door has been opened, and many investigators are now working alongside government law-enforcement agencies, and are seen as an important arm of the establishment's fight against crime and corruption.

The history
of private investigation

It is difficult to know exactly when the first private investigator appeared. If we think of investigators as an arm of the police, then we have to look back at least as far as the early Egyptians and Sumerians. Spies have been around for several thousand years and therefore, it can be argued, that they have been the forerunners of today's investigators.

The early investigators were part-time keepers of the peace, especially in the USA. Many companies employed talented individuals who worked to locate and bring criminals to justice; in this cause, they often took on work that could not be handled by the established police force. Consequently many of today's investigators in the USA will have a case load which includes murder, extortion and other high-profile crimes. In Great Britain the work is as varied, but private investigators will have a case load which is predominately made up of matrimonial, divorce and civil matters, with an occasional high-profile crime thrown in.

Private investigators in both countries will be made up of former police officers, ex-military operators, former insurance-company assessors and individuals who have drifted into the civilian spy game. Over recent years, however, there has been an increase in the formation of training organisations that will offer courses in investigation techniques, with successful participants earning a recognised professional qualification.

Basic techniques

Basic equipment

As a professional investigator, at the very least you should carry with you at all times a pencil, black ballpoint pen, small notebook, identification (real and assumed), pen-knife, pocket torch, mobile telephone, a decent watch and plenty of loose change. Along with these essential items, you should also have quick and easy access to a camera with a good-quality lens. Traditionally, this would have been a robust, metal-bodied 35mm camera fitted with a telephoto lens, with several other lenses close to hand that could easily be mounted should the need arise. The camera would be loaded with film at all times and several backup colour and black-and-white films carried offering a range of film speed.

Nowadays, there is no need to carry this amount of equipment around, as the modern digital camera is small enough to be concealed easily and operated in a wide variety of conditions without the need to use different lenses and film speeds to compensate for distance and ever-changing light levels. These remarkable cameras generally come equipped with a digital zoom facility, and can display the image on a small LCD screen immediately it has been taken. This enables an investigator to check that the image taken is good enough to prove the case, without having to retreat to a laboratory to develop the film.

Having satisfied himself regarding the quality of his work, the investigator can be confident about the shoot, and simply download the resulting images on to a computer and have the evidence e-mailed to the client within minutes.

The same can be said for the digital video camera. At one time, you would have had to take a friend along with you just to carry the battery pack. Now the digital video camera is small enough to use with one hand, and has a long battery life. Once again, this equipment

PICTURE 1

*The digital camera is ideal
for use by the P.I.*

*Video cameras are small enough
to be easily concealed*

allows an operator to view the image at any time. The film can be paused at an important point, so that any interesting event can be chosen and the image either freeze-framed to draw attention to it, or a still print can be taken from it and the image used to support witness statements or reports.

Having said this, it is still good practice to be able to use the older, more established equipment as you may well have to revert to it when engaged on lengthy assignments — especially in areas where recharging a battery is impossible, or some other unforeseen circumstance dictates. When working in some developing countries and within Eastern European war zones, I have had to revert to my investigative roots and not only been forced to use old camera equipment, but also to develop negatives and prints using very primitive laboratory facilities and home-made chemical developers.

Binoculars have also undergone a great deal of change in recent years, and are much smaller than they used to be. Most modern pairs are fitted with very effective, easily operated zoom adjustment. Those offering night vision are best, and should always be carried with you in your vehicle, out of their carrying case and in such a position that allows you to utilise them quickly.

Although I've already mentioned that a notepad and pen form a very important part of an investigator's basic, essential kit, sometimes it isn't practicable to make a written record of significant events. In situations when you as an investigator cannot be overheard, such as when following someone in your car, it may be better and safer to use a small voice-operated recorder so that you can give a second-by-second account as the investigation progresses. Obviously you cannot carry all of this around with you all of the time, but at the very least you should carry a pen, pencil and notebook even when working undercover.

In such operating conditions, it is sometimes necessary to hide the notebook, emergency money and proper ID in the lining of clothing or attached to the body. It is not sufficient to stuff them down your socks, as during any activity the socks may slip or an item may slide under your foot, making it hard to walk or run. It is essential to secure items such as these.

Imagine yourself in a covert situation, listening to and watching a gang of thieves as you work alongside them. Suddenly, your sock slips and out pours your gadgets for all to see like a bungling magician's tricks. At best, your incompetence will be embarrassing, while in the worst case you could even lose your life. Just above the ankle and slightly to the rear of the leg is a good place to secure any items, but take care that they are secured to your leg in such a way that they do not dig into your flesh.

A watch is an extremely important piece of an investigator's equipment, and should be chosen with care. A small dial using diamonds for the hours may look good, but it is totally impracticable in an operational situation. The ideal choice is a simple, quality timepiece with large luminous numerals and hands displaying easily readable day and date that is both water- and shock-proof – the simpler the better. Whistle-blowing, flag-waving, multi-digital watches giving the time in 20 different countries – whether or not an expensive make – will be of little use when you are on an extended surveillance operation in cramped and dark conditions. Besides, if you do get into trouble, this type of watch will be the first thing that will be taken from you, and could easily give your cover away.

You should also carry a lightweight compass, and be proficient in using it. Knowing where you are, and in what direction particular objects lie relative to your position, is important – especially when you are on a surveillance job or trying to identify the location of a drug-dealing gang's lair in a remote corner of the world.

Having the ability to quickly contact your 'buddy' (team colleague), office or client is a definite bonus. A good-quality mobile telephone is a relatively inexpensive item that not only keeps you in touch, but can be a lifesaver. Wherever possible, program in the number of your buddy or the local police so that they can be quickly summoned in an emergency.

I can recall one occasion when I was working in the heart of

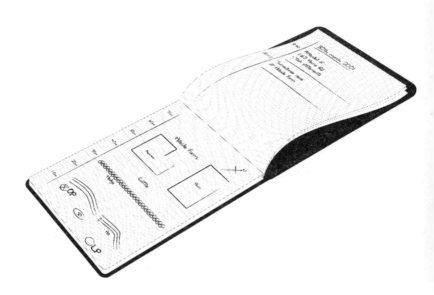

*Essential equipment for the P.I.
is the investigator notebook*

PICTURE 4

*The P.I.'s watch should be accurate, functional
and easily read night and day*

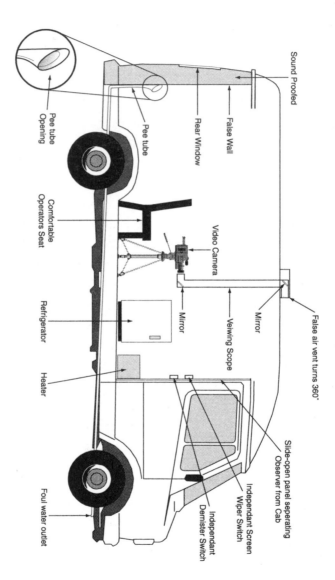

A purpose built surveillance vehicle is expensive in the beginning but becomes cost effective if you are involved in a lot of covert surveillance operations

Sound Proofed

False Wall

Rear Window

Pee tube

Pee tube Opening

Comfortable Operators Seat

Refrigerator

Heater

Foul water outlet

Video Camera

Mirror

Veiwing Scope

Mirror

False air vent turns 360°

Slide-open panel seperating Observer from Cab

Independant Screen Wiper Switch

Independant Demister Switch

PICTURE 5

Birmingham, England, when during an investigation I came into contact with a very violent man. I had already programmed 999 (the UK number for the emergency services), into my mobile and simply pressed the Send key and the call was answered immediately. I was very relieved, although somewhat surprised when the operator who took the call told me she was in the Glasgow exchange in Scotland – 300 hundred miles from my problem. However, she put my mind at rest by explaining that the emergency system finds the next available operator, no matter where that operator was in the UK, and this operator then contacts the police local to the call. Sure enough, within ten minutes police officers from the Birmingham division arrived and took the man away.

Another excellent communication aid for keeping you in touch with the rest of the world is an up-to-date computer with Internet capability. This is a very important piece of equipment and should not be overlooked. As well as enabling you to use the computer's word-processing capability to produce professional reports, the computer will also allow you to access and utilise a variety of databases.

One other vital piece of equipment without which an investigator would not be able to do their job is a reliable vehicle. Ideally, this should be a saloon car, fitted with surveillance and tracking equipment. However, the vehicle colour and type are very important. For example, a bright or unusual colour stands out and is easily recognisable, making it virtually useless in a surveillance role. Models with special features that draw people's attention to them should also be avoided, along with flashy or personalised registration numbers, extra lights and other 'go-faster' accessories.

Central locking and electric windows will come in handy as safety features, should you find yourself in a tricky situation. A sunroof will allow enough light in to enable you to write notes or consult maps without having to turn on the interior light during the hours of darkness. Another benefit of the sunroof is its use as an extra observation window to allow you to view high-rise buildings without having to stretch your neck out of the vehicle's side windows.

If you and your team of investigators are going to be involved in a surveillance role on a regular basis, then it may be worthwhile fitting out a purpose-built vehicle with all the equipment needed to undertake static and mobile surveillance. I have often used this type of vehicle, and although it does have its limitations it is well worth the investment.

As with the car, a purpose-built surveillance vehicle should be of a type that can blend in anywhere. It should be in a neutral colour with no flashy extras. Ideally, it should be large enough for a man to stand up in, or at least to sit in comfortably for long periods. There is nothing more demoralising than having to work cramped in a vehicle for hours without being able to stretch your muscles.

The vehicle should be fitted with a panel between the driver and the surveillance operating area so that anyone passing by will not be able to see into the back. Darkened windows are not really an option, because although they hide the occupants from the outside world, they look suspicious and can compromise the vehicle's use. Rear windows are worth having, although they should be small so as not to appear too conspicuous. They should be obstructed by hanging work clothing over them from the inside, or by stacking a selection of boxes in such a way that they obscure a curious observer's view, but still allow a hidden hand-held camera to be used for filming activity outside.

The inside of the vehicle should be sound-proofed using dark material. Carpeting on the floor, sides and roof will cut down on noise, and will also have the added benefit of keeping the vehicle relatively warm and absorbing some of the moisture, which will always threaten to cover your observation positions with condensation. Fitting a second battery with a switch-over facility operated from the surveillance position can save draining your main engine battery. This slave battery can be used to keep the vehicle's demisting system working on a very low setting, thus creating as little noise as possible so as not to arouse suspicion.

There should also be a facility for operating the windscreen wipers from the slave battery. Using the wipers may give your position away, but when it is raining you may have no choice. Faced with this potential 'give-away' hazard, use them sparingly. When you do need to clear the windscreen, check the immediate area around the vehicle and wait until another vehicle passes by before operating them. The presence of the other vehicle will help to lessen the visual impact of the moving wipers and also mask the noise. If it is snowing, forget it and try another day as there is no bigger give-away than a parked vehicle covered in snow with the windscreen cleared!

The best method for avoiding detection is to fit a periscope, which looks through an air vent on the top of the vehicle. One drawback with it is that you are limited by its inability to view any events close to the vehicle, and by its rigid fixing which may stop you from smoothly following any action. A combination of hand-held and fixed cameras will give you the best of both worlds. The vehicle should also be fitted with the team's radio command system, so that if it is used in a protracted surveillance role it can act as the operational headquarters (HQ). A top-of-the-range custom-built surveillance vehicle must be properly fitted with electronic tracking systems, along with covert audio and video receivers and recorders.

Spending time in such vehicles isn't easy, and it helps if they are fitted with a small heater for cold days and a cooling fan for hot ones. A compact refrigerator stocked with plenty of cold drinks and chocolate may seem like a luxury but, believe me, it is necessary.

Last, but by no means least, is the incorporation of a 'pee tube'. This is a simple contraption consisting of a large funnel with a long tube that can either end in a plastic container secured to the underside of the vehicle or be discharged by the offside front wheel. Obviously, never use this facility when there is a risk that the exiting urine can be seen pouring from the vehicle – wait until there is no-one around, and then use it. The urine will inevitably leave a puddle, but it will look as though your radiator has been leaking and won't attract anyone's suspicion. Someone may leave a message on the windscreen telling the 'absent' driver that he has a problem, but other than this there is nothing to indicate a team at work. Water exiting from the rear of the vehicle would give rise to suspicion, however, as there is no logical reason for liquid to be there.

On occasions, you may have to work undercover in locations such as clubs, bars, shops and factories. Recording times and events in these situations can be difficult, but it's made easier by using good-quality, well-concealed equipment. If you constantly look at your watch or write notes in a club, you will soon draw attention to yourself, heightening suspicion and possibly giving the game away. A quick glance at your watch is probably all you can do to register a particular event and later you may be able to visit the toilet and access your notebook to make a proper recording.

The Pocket Notebook

It is not absolutely necessary to use a pocket notebook, but in my opinion it makes sense and goes some way to maintaining a professional approach towards the work of a private investigator.

Skill in writing reports and statements can only be achieved by practice, but whether skilful or not, you should exercise care at all times so that any written work is accurate, legible, clear in its meaning and strictly to the point. Much of your report writing will follow the notes you make in your pocket notebook. These are known in the trade as contemporaneous notes, and are admissible in legal proceedings. I would suggest that if you do decide to use a pocket notebook, you follow the simple rules adhered to by most law-enforcement agencies.

The notebook should be small enough to be carried and concealed easily. It should consist of lined paper with a left-hand ruled margin in which to log times. Having said this, I happen to prefer small graph paper, as this makes the book much more versatile.

The object of the notebook is to record your first-hand knowledge of an occurrence, thereby providing you with a basis for the completion of a written or verbal report at a later time. If you are going to use a pocket notebook, carry it at all times and properly record all information soon after the occurrence concerned.

Accuracy is the most important aspect of a professional investigator's life. All entries should be made in the pocket notebook:

At the time of the occurrence
or
As soon as is practicable after the occurrence or offence.

This ensures that the recordings are as accurate as possible, and accuracy is more likely when events are fresh in the writer's mind. By taking this approach, you will be able to refer to your notebook entry if your recollection is challenged in court.

As a general guideline, all written recordings should show the day and date in capitals, and should also be underlined to indicate a new entry. All recorded names should also be in capitals.

Report writing and statement taking

R eports take different forms depending on the subject matter. The compilation of reports is a skill that's acquired by practice and guidance. Throughout, take care to ensure that your written work is accurate, legible, clear and to the point. Often, people use their own short-hand when under pressure, believing that they will be able to fill in the gaps at a later time. In practice, when I've fallen into this trap, I have sat down ready to transcribe my notes, only to be faced with poor handwriting and gaps that make no real sense. Relying on one's memory in such situations is a recipe for a disastrous report.

Reports usually fall into one of three main categories: administrative memoranda concerning policy procedures or personal matters; occurrence reports, which provide a written record of an event, but which may not require any further action (such as a simple progress report for your client); or reports which detail an offence or occurrence, including formal statements from witnesses, the accused or an expert.

Construction

Most reports, in whatever form, will contain the following essential details:

- The identification and details of the relevant experience of the author
- The date of compilation
- To whom it is addressed
- The heading describing the subject
- And, finally, the author's signature and relevant qualifications at the end.

When writing a report, ensure that you include the following as a minimum:

- Day, date and time of the occurrence, offence, etc.
- Exact location
- Identity of the persons concerned
- Description of events
- How it came to your/their notice
- Action taken
- Any direct speech given as an explanation or witnessed
- In the case of an allegation of an offence, the exact offence in law

PRACTICE SESSION

Take an everyday event, such as a shopping trip or a visit to a local place of interest. During the trip, write down significant parts of the event in your pocket notebook using the investigator's accepted form. Have a friend or investigation colleague go with you to act as an observer.

Two or three days after the trip, write a full report using your notes, give it to your buddy to read, and ask them to comment honestly on the report content and on how well it explained the actual events.

Try this on a number of occasions, using your buddy's constructive criticism to improve your reporting skills.

Video surveillance log

A dedicated log is essential when gathering evidence by surveillance methods, especially video evidence. All recording equipment should be checked before you use it to ensure that the correct date and time are properly displayed. If you are fortunate enough to be able to speak directly into the microphone as you are filming, then this is the best option. Be careful what you do say though, as the film and its sound could be used in evidence and listened to by all sorts of people.

It is usually better to have at least two people in this type of surveillance situation – one to do the filming, and the other to record the events manually in the log. The events must obviously be recorded accurately, stating the time and what was recorded and by whom.

PICTURE 6

Video Cassette No: 001   Time In | Time Out
                              22:00 | _____

OPERATION: Fireglow

Date & Time	Event	Loggist
28/2/01 22:00	Investigator 01 Recording	D. Hill
22:02	Male & Female approaching drug dealer (Target 2)	—"—
22:10	Money and drugs change hands	—"—
22:15	Male & Female leave area on foot	—"—
22:50	Adult Male approaches drug dealer	—"—
22:55	Adult Male leaves area *No exchange seen	—"—
23:00	Change operator Investigator 02 Recording	A. Byatt

Page 1

*An accurate record is essential especially
when it is used in legal proceedings*

Still photography

Sometimes it is more practical to take still photographs. Once again, a log must be kept to ensure that you remember the events as they occur in your photographic record. It is normal practice to number photographs on the reverse side, and to endorse each photograph with a statement indicating that the photograph has not been retouched or enhanced in any way, the statement then being dated and signed by the photographer.

File construction

As a case evolves, you will probably have a number of forms, which should be collated and made into a file. Although the forms will vary from case to case, the format of the file will be the same. The narrative in a report is really a summary of several sources of information, a copy of which is kept in the file along with other documents – such as copies of your pocket notebook entry, statements from witnesses, correspondence, lists of items of evidence or the facts behind a crime.

Taking Statements

One of the most important elements of all file construction is the inclusion of statements. The proper taking of statements is a skilled business which, when carried out professionally, not only helps to uncover the history of an occurrence or crime but goes some way to indicating the professionalism of the investigator.

In essence, statement-taking is an interview technique, relying on a professional approach and good-quality questions. Before meeting to interview the witness and taking the statement, familiarise yourself with the background to the case. Get a description of the events in general terms so that you can move the interview on to very specific details at an appropriate stage. Find out who was involved, what happened, where it happened, when it happened and how the witness was involved. Avoid hearsay evidence – in other words, your witness should have a first-hand account. You should only record information they gained from their senses – they can tell you what they saw, what they heard, what they felt, what they touched or what they could smell. You should not include what someone else told them they could see, hear, feel, touch or smell.

At the start of the interview, introduce yourself clearly; explain what you are there for and that you have experience of taking statements. Do not lead the witness into saying things that you want to hear – let them do the talking. Never promise any specific outcome to your time with them or their statement. Spend time settling and relaxing the witness. Going over the story briefly before taking the actual statement is a good way of settling down, and allows you the opportunity to gather your thoughts. It will also help if you acknowledge that there is an agenda and yours is to get a true account in the words of the witness, whereas the agenda of the witness may well be to find out the implications of making a statement. They may be fearful of the consequences, especially if they are likely to be called to court. In some circumstances, they may even be afraid of reprisals and ask about protection.

It is most important to allow a witness to go back over the events, as this improves the quality of the statement. Try to get them to trust you, but acknowledge that they may be wary, under pressure or scared.

Questions

Closed questions

The way in which you ask questions will either help or hinder a witness. Avoid closed questions that can be answered with yes or no, or where the answer invited is short or limited. For example: 'Did you see it?' 'You've been there before, haven't you?' 'Do you like her?' As you can see, closed questions do not encourage nervous, shy, anxious or withdrawn people to expand their reply. One-word answers stem the flow of the conversation, and therefore limit the information you'll receive. Asking closed questions implies that you are taking control of the conversation, and doesn't allow the other person any space in which to expand or introduce items they may want to tell you about.

Open questions

An open question gives the witness a choice about the way in which they answer. Open questions often start with 'how' or 'why': 'How did you see it?' 'Why were you there?' 'What did you like about her?' The person answering is invited to give more information. Generally, questions beginning with 'how' tend to feel less inquisitorial than those beginning with 'why', which can make people feel that they have to justify or defend their statement.

Reflective questions

Questions can sometimes be asked that qualify or reflect what is being said, and allow you to ensure that you fully understand the meaning in a statement. For example, the witness may say, 'I liked being with him,' which could be rephrased by you as: 'You enjoyed his company then?' or, 'I went to the bar,' could be rephrased as, 'You went to buy a drink?' This technique can serve to confirm your interest and invite further discussion.

Leading questions

These must be avoided at all costs, as leading questions lead the witness. Suggesting an answer, or implying that you know what has happened, will prevent you from getting a first-hand account of what really has happened. 'Was David in the bar?' should be rephrased as: 'Did you know anyone in the bar?'

Too many questions

Bombarding a witness with questions can be counter-productive, and will stop the flow of conversation. Once you have asked a question, leave it up to the witness to answer – do not interrupt them in mid-flow. When they have finished, ask the next question slowly and deliberately, keeping your questions short and focused.

Irrelevant questions

If it isn't important, then don't ask it. For example, if the witness says, 'I walked into the garden,' don't ask what the flowers were like – unless the flowers are important, of course.

Statements rely on people's memory. Age, mental illness, stress and trauma will all have an effect on memory. Long delays between the event and the recollection of the witness will lead to some memory loss, although accuracy regarding details is usually still very good.

A witness is not always the person who saw an event. A witness may be a person who can describe goods or property. A person may have seen someone carrying a stolen item or running away from a scene, without knowing the full extent of the problem, but they can give a description of a person, or a vehicle. A private investigator may have interviewed or met with a suspect, or have information which can help the case. All will have information that will help paint a picture and assist with the investigation.

As a police officer, I used a witness statement form that complied with laws and rules that were acceptable to courts and could be used in evidence. Private investigators can and should use similar forms which, likewise, will be acceptable to the court. When working alongside the police, it is usual for them to use their forms throughout. When compiling statements, keep the writing in the place provided and on one side of the paper only. The exception to this is where you put the address of a witness on the reverse of the first page, so that when copies are given out the address is not visible.

Every statement must include a signed declaration about its truth and accuracy, and the witness must sign the bottom of each page. Witnesses may write the statement for themselves or, if they prefer, someone else (usually the investigator) may write it for them. If someone else writes it, a declaration must be made to indicate that the witness has read the statement before signing. It should be noted that there is no legal obligation on any person to provide a written statement. A good approach in the beginning will often gain the co-operation of the witness to supply a written statement. Where a witness refuses to give you a statement, you should note this down in your pocket notebook and inform whoever is instructing you as soon as possible.

Remember that a statement should be in the words of the person making it. It should identify the person and indicate that person's connection with the offence, occurrence, or whatever. It should be a description of first-hand knowledge, and should describe events in a chronological order. It should also be to the point, with any amendments or alterations being struck through with a single line and initialled. It must be the witness's account only. Nothing should be in the statement that has been suggested or put there by anyone other than the witness. A witness should not be encouraged to change their account in favour of the thoughts of the investigator or some other person.

PRACTICE SESSION

Review the contents of the statement taker's introduction.

Practice your introduction. Taking an audio recording and reviewing it may help you to feel comfortable with it.

Use your buddy or a member of your family who has had a recent event such as a special meeting, accident or some other similar episode.

Try out your introduction on them.

Follow this with an interview about their event.

When you are satisfied that you have an idea of the story from the interview, take a proper statement.

At the end, ask the storyteller to read the statement.

Now ask them to comment on the accuracy of the content, and on whether or not they would be willing to sign it as a true record if it were used in a court of law.

Camera and video

The era of digital imagery is upon us, making historical recording easier and of higher quality than ever before. The drawback is the cost, but for those who can afford it, the sky really is the limit. For the rest of us, a good-quality 35mm camera – preferably one that has a metal body, zoom lens and which can easily be operated with cold hands – will be sufficient.

If you have only an elementary knowledge of photography, you may well benefit from taking a photography course. Having said that, the kind of course you're likely to find will not fully equip you for the type of photography you'll need in the private-investigation field.

During my training, I spent a great deal of time on this subject, learning to take and develop photographs in all types of locations and in different conditions, including taking photographs in complete darkness using infrared film and light. Photography is an extremely interesting subject which, once mastered, can produce amazing results. In essence, though, as long as you can take a decent photograph, you're in business.

I've already mentioned the benefits of the modern digital camera. Although the following information is primarily intended for use with a standard 35mm single-lens reflex (SLR) camera, it can improve your overall ability and should be used as the basis for quality camera work.

All traditional cameras work on the same simple principle. Basically, they consist of a lightproof box housing light-sensitive paper – the film. Films are coated with chemicals that react to light and form an image from the light. The type of chemical coating dictates the speed of the film and whether or not the film will be colour or black and white. Slow films react more slowly, and are best employed in taking pictures that need good contrast. Fast films react quickly and are best suited to action pictures; they are also more tolerant of error.

Film speed is expressed in American Standard Authority units, commonly known as the film's ASA value. Normal film speeds range

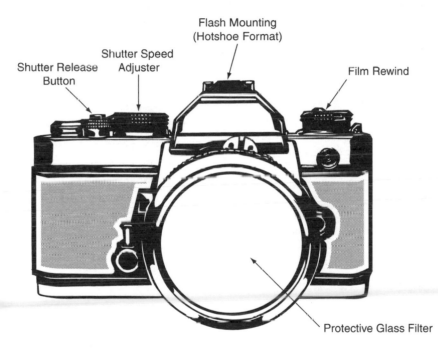

The 35mm SLR is an ideal camera for the P.I.
especially when it has large operating buttons

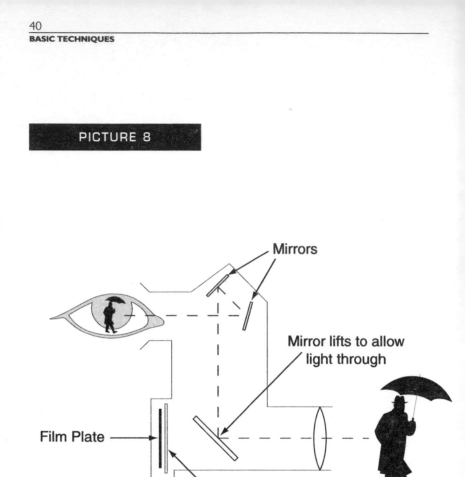

The single lens reflex allows the photographer to see exactly what the film will see by a series of mirrors

from around 25 ASA to 1000 ASA, but for the majority of an investigator's work, 400 ASA black and white or colour will be sufficient. Some films are specifically manufactured for use with infrared light, and therefore also has a place in the investigator's holdall.

There should be a good stock of film in the office. It is best to store film in a refrigerator, but it should be taken out well before it is used so that it can become acclimatised to current atmospheric conditions. At the end of a shoot, place used film back in the refrigerator if you are unable to get it developed straight away.

Film is stored on a roll, and once it has been loaded into the camera it stretches flat across the rear of the camera; this position is known as the film plane. When you wind on the film, it moves from left to right, the exposed film being stored on a spool that remains in the camera. Until the exposed film has been re-wound into the canister, It has no outer case to protect it, and therefore any light entering through the back of the camera will ruin the film and the shoot.

An SLR camera allows the photographer to look through the viewfinder and see the exact picture that will be recorded on the film. This is achieved by using a simple mirror positioned between the lens and the film, blocking the light and reflecting it through the viewfinder window. As the shutter-release button is pressed, the mirror automatically lifts out of the way, allowing light through and enabling the image to be recorded on the film behind. This type of camera allows the operator to change lenses according to requirements, and is ideal for an investigator.

Behind the mirror are two shutters: the primary and the secondary. They can be made from cloth or metal, and are known as the focal plane shutter. This focal plane shutter lies close to the film, effectively preventing any light from getting to the film. There is a gap between the shutters. As the picture is taken, these shutters chase across the film; the gap between them is variable and allows less or more light on to the film. This is known as the shutter speed. A slow shutter speed allows more time for the image to be seen by the film and is better in low light, but because it is open for longer it is susceptible to blurring. A fast shutter speed is best for moving subjects, and consequently is the preferred option for the private investigator. Shutter speed is expressed in fractions of a second from around 1/4000th to 1 second, automatically timed. Thereafter, there is a facility to hold the shutter open manually for as long as you wish.

The lens is the means by which light is gathered and organised to form a recognisable image on the film. Lenses are classified by their focal length, which is the distance of a perfectly focused image when the lens is set at infinity. Telephoto and zoom lenses give an investigator a better chance of obtaining photographs of a subject from a safe distance. However, these lenses can be heavy and difficult to control with blurred images caused by camera shake a common problem. A wide range of tripods is available to provide a stable camera platform, and they should be used at every possible opportunity. Unfortunately, an investigator does not always have the luxury of ideal working conditions, so it is important to practice and master camera handling in difficult circumstances.

Photography in poor light conditions is another technique that needs to be practised and fully understood. Using a conventional flash-gun is definitely a non-starter – the exception probably being when you are in a nightclub or bar, and need to take a photograph of a couple in a compromising position. In this case, you could use a normal snapshot camera and flash and set up your buddy to pose for a 'shot for the family album' – making sure the actual subjects are in the background frame, of course.

In poor light conditions, you can fit an attachment to the camera that acts in the same way as a passive night viewer by amplifying any existing light. The problem is that they have an eerie green tint, and fine detail is not very good.

In complete darkness, you need to resort to active night viewing, which involves the use of infrared film and light. In essence, as we've said already, a camera and film works by light; white light is the norm.

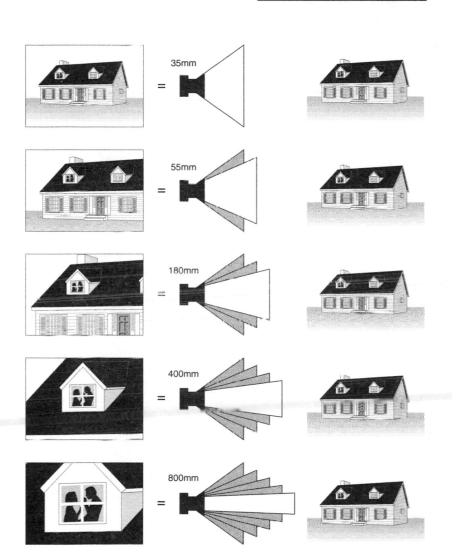

Choosing the right lens for the job is a very important
aspect of the P.I's photographic skill

PICTURE 10

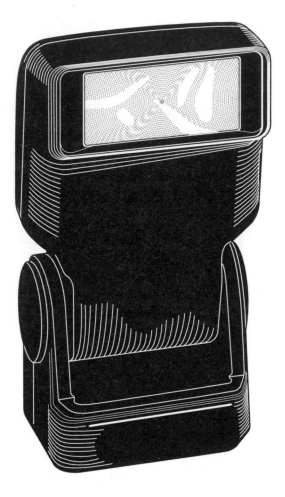

Covering a standard flash with an infra-red filter will enable you to take photographs in complete darkness

*To illuminate a large area with infra-red light use
a hand held search light and cover the lens with
military vehicle infra-red light filter*

However, white light requires a flash in dark conditions, and this is not conducive to covert operation. Infrared light is undetectable to the human eye and is the obvious choice but, unfortunately, it is useless with normal film. Infrared-sensitive film can be purchased from most reputable photographic dealers. Once it has been loaded, you can use a normal flash attachment by covering the light with an infrared filter. You won't see the flash, but the film will, and it will take very good pictures.

The problem is that you will not be able to see the target without a night viewing aid. These are widely available, but are cumbersome and impracticable for the photographer. The best way of getting around this problem is to pre-set the camera – you will have to practice to get the hang of it. Start with a wide-angle lens and set it at infinity. Adjust the flash to a setting that corresponds to this distance. These settings should give you a decent photograph at a distance of up to around 25ft.

Once you have mastered this technique, you will need to practice close-up photography. You can do this by using a measuring stick, which can be held on the body of the camera and will keep it in perfect focus, even though you cannot see through the viewfinder. The only way to master the best distances for your camera and flash is by trial and error. Once you know the best settings, mark the camera so that you can feel them without having to try to look at them.

In wide, open spaces such as in a close observation position, it is possible to illuminate a large area with the use of a powerful hand-held flashlight and a military headlight infrared filter.

Because infrared film is sensitive to red light, it cannot be properly developed in a normal darkroom. You will either have to locate a technician who is used to dealing with this type of equipment, or you will have to learn to operate your camera and develop your film in complete darkness.

Much of the photography work you undertake as an investigator will involve being outdoors, often in poor weather conditions. Keeping your equipment in good working order therefore has to be a priority. Portability and ease of access are the criteria you should observe. You and your camera should be constantly at the ready as many a good opportunity has been lost because an investigator stowed the camera in an inaccessible part of his baggage. Obviously, you can't walk around all the time with a camera and an 800mm lens strapped to your neck, so you should think about the best way of getting your kit to the area of operation.

Some jobs, however, such as taking photographs of accident sites, will allow you to carry your equipment openly. Other jobs will be of a covert nature, and as such you will have to ensure in these circumstances that you can carry and operate your camera without being seen. Carrying your camera, lenses and films with you requires waterproof clothing incorporating plenty of pockets, including extra-large ones. When there is no alternative, you may have to carry everything to the operations area in a rucksack; this should be in a dark colour – large enough to carry everything you need – and have several external pockets with quick-release straps. The camera, ready to use, must be in one of these external pockets.

Some surveillance operations will have to be approached as a sniper approaches his quarry. Moving into a good observation position takes time and patience. A short strap should safely secure the camera across the body, pushed to the rear so that it can be retrieved quickly when needed. Hanging it around your neck as a tourist would do is of no use, as it will swing around and become a hazard.

One of the most vulnerable parts of a camera is the lens face. Clear glass filters that can be screwed onto the front of all your lenses are the most effective protection. Generally speaking, water and cameras don't mix – unless it's an underwater camera, of course. Most good-quality cameras will have some resistance to a little water, but waterproof covers for cameras are available that can be used if there is a likelihood of severe weather.

Using a camera in outdoor surveillance operations will inevitably expose it to a high degree of dust and dirt. Any debris that gets into the body of the camera will cause problems. You must therefore avoid opening the camera, except when you need to change films. Placing the camera in a clean polythene sack (preferably black) before opening it will cut down on any contamination. Extreme weather conditions will also cause problems with a camera and film – too much heat is likely to affect the film, while cold temperatures can cause the camera's mechanical parts to become sluggish in operation. In freezing conditions, the film may also become very brittle.

Passing through security screening, especially at airports, can be a tricky business. Exposed film may be damaged as it is scanned with electronic detectors. Where possible, ask the security staff to check it through by hand. Sometimes they will, sometimes they will not, but think about this aspect before you decide to go through security.

On some assignments, it may be better to have the film developed in the area of operations. I was in Albania in the mid-1980s and had to buy film locally. Having carried out the operation, I returned to the UK with five rolls of undeveloped film. I handed it in to be developed, and was told that it needed a special type of developer that the laboratory did not have. It took me two weeks and a great deal of extra expense to discover the correct formula.

The information given above for handling a 35mm camera also applies to video cameras. Video cameras offer you the opportunity to present your client with a film of whatever action you witnessed. Digital cameras are small enough to conceal, yet give wonderful results. The same operating principles apply as for still photography – you need a camera that can withstand the rigours of use in adverse conditions, and which has large operating buttons and switches. It is also worth investing in a video camera that can record with or without sound, while low light settings and at least a 100x zoom are a must.

On occasions, I have been hidden behind a black cloth in the rear of a van, filming through a tear in the cloth. If I had been using a camera with automatic focus, the camera would have focused on the surrounding cloth and even with a large tear, the camera will still focus on the windscreen wipers, steering wheel, rear-view mirror. In fact, anything other than the distant target. Needless to say, ensure you use a camera that enables you to disable the auto focus.

Night-viewing equipment

Equipment that allows you to see at night is widely available. There are many designs, offering a range of options at reasonable prices. Night-viewing equipment falls into two categories: active and passive.

The active type uses its own light source, an infrared beam, which cannot be seen by the human eye. This has the obvious benefit of being able to be used in total darkness. Passive optical equipment, on the other hand, works by amplifying all available light, such as that from the moon, stars and street lights. The drawback with active equipment is that it can only be used for short-range filming, and can also be seen by anyone using an infrared scope.

Night-viewing equipment has been specifically developed for military and security use. Over recent years, however, much of the equipment has found its way on to domestic markets, and is now available in many stores.

Electronic aids

In the world of the investigator and the spy, the word 'bug' is used to describe a variety of covert electronic listening and viewing devices, ranging from simple miniature voice recorders to sophisticated micro transmitters capable of sending sound and vision across the world. There are literally thousands of these devices in everyday use, and many of them are used illegally.

However, their legality varies from country to country, and even from state to state in the USA. If you are considering using this type of equipment, make sure that you check on its use in the area of operations before you proceed. A lucrative 'safe' area for the private investigator is in the detection of these devices. Electronic scanning equipment used to locate bugs is expensive to buy, but is in great demand.

Electronic surveillance

In the UK, there are extensive restrictions on the use of electronic surveillance equipment. In essence, the Wireless and Telegraphy Act 1949 makes it an offence to use a radio transmitter without a license, and the Telecommunications Act 1984 and its amendments – along with the Interception of Communications Act – lists numerous offences in respect of the 'tapping' of telephones and interfering with equipment and communications.

In the US, there are also extensive restrictions on the use of electronic surveillance equipment. In essence, the Electronic Communications Privacy Act of 1986 makes it a crime for anyone to intercept or disclose wire, oral, or electronic communications (the Communications Assistance to Law Enforcement Act, however, grants slightly different laws to Federal Authorities). US law does prohibit manufacturing, distribution, possession and advertising of communication interception devices, but both the devices and "make your own" plans are widely available on the internet. Restrictions on both the devices and their use vary by country.

Although these restrictions are in place, equipment is widely available through legitimate retail outlets. In fact, there are very few restrictions on the sale of electronic 'bugging' equipment. To list all the relevant legislation is beyond the scope of this book, but I strongly advise you to take legal advice regarding the restrictions currently in force in the countries in which you will be working.

Despite such restrictions, as a professional investigator you should be familiar with all types of equipment, their availability and their working characteristics. You may be approached to work in a country with few restrictions and, consequently, you would be expected to know about the equipment best suited to a particular job. Likewise, in countries with stringent regulations, you may be asked to carry out 'de-bugging' work and, once again, you would be expected to know where bugs are liable to be positioned and be familiar with the types used. With this in mind, we shall now look at bugs and their use.

Perhaps the simplest of all the devices used for eavesdropping is the audiocassette recorder. These well-known and proven machines come in all shapes and sizes, and can be purchased cheaply from a multitude of outlets. Tiny digital models with voice-activated recording are easy to use and conceal. Using the voice-activated mode will prolong tape life and, consequently, reduce the number of times the tape will have to be changed.

PICTURE 12

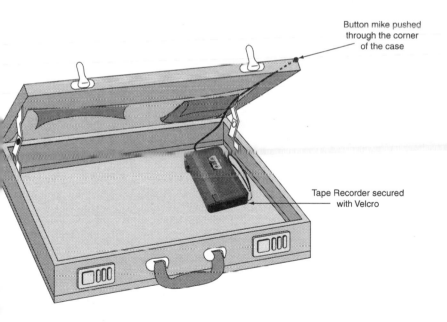

Button mike pushed through the corner of the case

Tape Recorder secured with Velcro

With a little effort you can easily adapt a standard briefcase to double as a covert recorder

However, there are several drawbacks with this type of device:

- The tape has to be changed at regular intervals
- The voice-activation mode cannot distinguish between the voice you want to record and any other voices
- Ambient noise can also cause the device to slip into record mode with the result being a tape full of everything but the conversation you wanted
- The batteries do not last long when used in this type of activity; plugging the recorder into the mains supply allows continual play, but is difficult to achieve covertly

These problems can be overcome to some extent, however. For example, you can overcome ambient noise with the use of a button microphone, which you can buy. The use of a wire allows the recorder to be placed some distance away from the target area, although generally a wire that is too long will lessen the effectiveness of the recorder. Nevertheless, with practice you will be able to determine the optimum working distance. These button microphones are very small, extremely sensitive and easily concealed. With a little thought and ingenuity, you can adapt the equipment for use as a body-worn system built into the body of a pen or integrated into a briefcase or other luggage.

Although it is quite acceptable to use primitive devices, they do limit the work you can carry out, and can let you down when you least expect it.

One of the most commonly used pieces of purpose-built kit is the recording briefcase. The majority of them are equipped with the latest in micro recording technology. The best ones are fitted with soundproofing that masks any noise from the integrated recorder. They are also fitted with very sensitive microphones that have the ability to pick up whispered speech with wonderful clarity. The best in the range can be operated remotely and will record continually for around three hours.

Other more sophisticated 'hard-wired' applications include long-range systems that use existing wiring as a carrier, and even

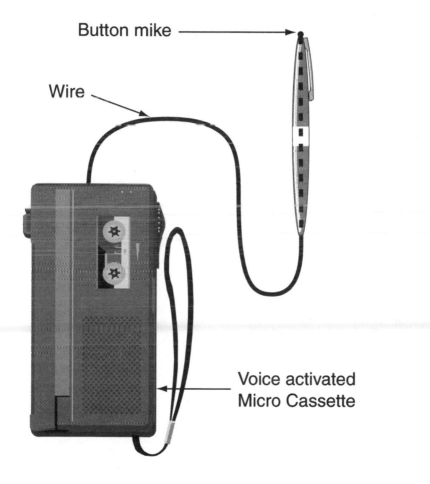

Button mike

Wire

Voice activated
Micro Cassette

*Another simply made covert recording device
is the recording pen*

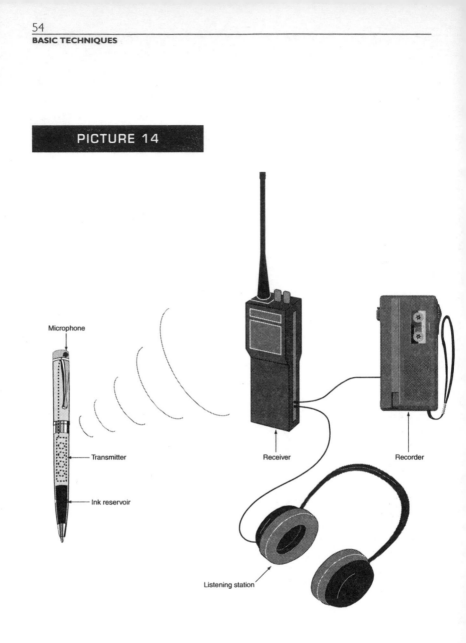

PICTURE 14

Microphone

Transmitter

Ink reservoir

Receiver

Recorder

Listening station

Although equipment that radiates a signal is easier to detect electronically non-wired equipment can be more versatile

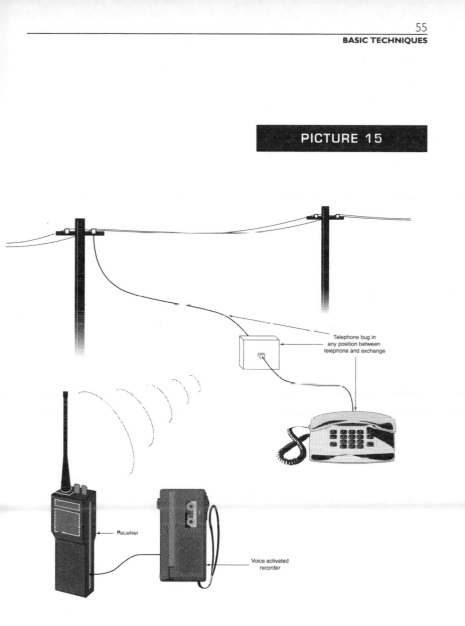

PICTURE 15

Telephone bug in
any position between
telephone and exchange

Receiver

Voice activated
recorder

*The telephone is often a great source of information.
Listening in is one way of gaining vital information*

conducting paint that can be used to form a continual electronic path across wall surfaces.

The above systems are fully integrated in that the listening device and recording facility are linked by wire. The benefit of this type of system is the difficulty in detecting them. Because they are non-radiating, they are impossible to find using conventional electronic sweeping equipment. Obviously, they can be found, but discovery can be a long job, as the only sure way is physically to look for them.

Sooner or later, a job will come in that cannot be tackled by integrated kit. When this happens, the best option is to look at equipment that is based on a transmitter and receiver. There are literally thousands of designs and specifications – certainly too many to cover in a book of this nature. There is a core of basic equipment in everyday use that can be easily purchased ready for use.

The pen bug is an interesting and widely used covert microphone and transmitter. It looks like any ordinary ballpoint pen, and even has an ink reservoir so that it can be used as a proper pen. With a range of up to around a quarter of a mile, this device can be left in a room and will monitor any conversations without drawing the slightest attention to its real purpose. It is a useful tool for the operator who is undercover and involved in meetings and discussions. The remote receiver can be linked to a recording system, allowing limitless playback of important details.

Microphones and transmitters can be built into virtually anything – a normal working calculator, for example. Given as a present, or simply left in the office, this device will continue to monitor conversations and transmit them to a listening station.

Telephone conversations can reveal a great deal in a very short space of time. Whether hard-wired or transmitted, there is equipment for every eventuality. They can easily be fitted anywhere between the telephone and the exchange; wire tapping is widely used, and can be left in place for long periods, because the bugs are powered by the telephone cable itself.

A picture is worth a thousand words, so the saying goes. But in the

PICTURE 16

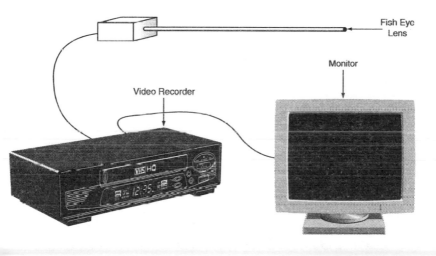

Fish Eye Lens

Monitor

Video Recorder

Inserting a probe through a wall allows investigators to film events in adjacent buildings

investigation game, a good picture is worth much more, especially if it's a moving picture! Like audio, visual recording equipment has seen a great deal of development in recent years. Micro cameras capable of working in extremely low light levels, coupled with reliable and powerful transmitters, enable visual signals to be transported anywhere in the world.

For the investigator, visual recording equipment can be built into any number of everyday items. Once again, the suitcase and other hand luggage can be used to film your suspect covertly; hand-held kit is difficult to use, especially in unfamiliar surroundings. Filming at eye level is the ideal method, but you would soon be compromised if you walked around with a briefcase perched on your shoulder. One way around this is to use vision-recording spectacles. The camera is concealed in the frame and either records straight onto a video recorder or the signal can be transmitted to a remote recorder.

On occasions, you may need to film events in an adjacent room. The best way of doing this is to infiltrate the area using a probe – a tiny long tube on the end of which is a fish-eye lens. These are virtually undetectable, relatively inexpensive and can help to move an investigation on very quickly.

The most basic equipment for the investigator to use and master is the two-way radio. The equipment may vary, but its use is universal and all operators should be familiar with proper radio and voice procedures. In our everyday face-to-face communication, we rely not only on our hearing but also on a person's body language and lip movements. Even if we miss the odd word, both of these factors help us to keep up with a conversation.

With radio communication, however, these two important aids to communication are missing; therefore it is most important that we communicate efficiently with the minimum of error. When you first start to communicate by radio, you will find it difficult to keep up with conversations. With practice, though, you will develop a 'radio ear', which is honed by constant use and allows you to interpret quickly what is being said. Because voice radio communication relies solely on hearing,

A = Alpha	**N = November**
B = Bravo	**O = Oscar**
C = Charlie	**P = Papa**
D = Delta	**Q = Quebec**
E = Echo	**R = Romeo**
F = Foxtrot	**S = Sierra**
G = Golf	**T = Tango**
H = Hotel	**U = Uniform**
I = India	**V = Victor**
J = Juliet	**W = Whisky**
K = Kilo	**X = X-ray**
L = Lima	**Y = Yankee**
M = Mike	**Z = Zulu**

operators use the phonetic alphabet to assist in complicated exchanges so that words can be spelt out without being mis-heard. Private investigators should learn this alphabet until it becomes second nature.

Precise, slow and deliberate pronunciation will also lessen the chance of a radio message being misunderstood. Radio operators should not use the radio for joking, or use unacceptable language. The golden rule is: if it's not important, then don't transmit it! Numbers should be announced and fully delivered. 0 should be delivered as zero. So a vehicle license number such as F012 ACO would be given as Foxtrot Zero One Two Alpha Charlie Oscar.

Operators should avoid using their name or their team names. My private investigation company is called Select Associates, so we use the call-sign SA, or Sierra Alpha. So, Sierra Alpha One would be the team leader, with SA2, SA3 and so on being the other operators. To cut down on 'air-time', codes are often used. These may vary from country to country or state to state, but the following is a widely recognised code consisting of 15 simple commands:

- **TEN ZERO**   Request 'talk through' for all radios to hear the message. [OK?]
- **TEN ONE**   Used when a call-sign comes back on duty after a rest or break. E.g. 'Base, Sierra One, Ten One, Received Over?'
- **TEN TWO**   Used when the call-sign arrives back at base.
- **TEN THREE**   Used to request a call-sign to return to base.
- **TEN FOUR**   Used to indicate that a message has been received and understood.
- **TEN FIVE**   Indicates that the call-sign is leaving the vehicle for a short time.
- **TEN SIX**   Used when the operator returns to the vehicle.
- **TEN SEVEN**   Used when a message needs to be repeated.
- **TEN EIGHT**   Used when you need to convey a message of a very confidential nature by different means.
- **TEN NINE**   Indicates that an operator is in need of immediate, emergency assistance.
- **TEN TEN**   Indicates that a call-sign is going

off duty, or taking a break.

- **TEN ELEVEN**   Used when a call-sign is moving out
of the operational area.
- **TEN TWELVE**   Indicates a return to the area
of operations.
- **TEN THIRTEEN**   Lets everyone know that the call-sign
is switching off his radio.
- **TEN FOURTEEN**   Given when the call-sign switches on
after a Ten Thirteen has been given

Having collected your radio from the stores, and having checked that it is fully charged and the correct channel has been selected, the next operation should be to check that is functioning correctly. This is done by simply calling your base or other users in the following way:

'*Sierra Alpha Base, Sierra Alpha One radio check, Over.*'
'*Sierra Alpha One received, Out.*'

Note that this is not a wordy conversation, but it is short and to the point. All radio communications should be exactly that – short, and to the point. If there is any doubt at all about the quality of the radio, then this should be dealt with before you begin an operation. A faulty radio – no matter how slight the fault – has no place on an operation. One thing is certain – a faulty radio will not get better with use!

On occasions, it may not be appropriate for you to speak into your radio, especially when undercover, or in the company of others who could compromise your operation in such circumstances. There is a recognised procedure, which involves answering questions by pressing the radio Send button. This can be heard by the receiving radio operator as a click:

One click = Yes
Two clicks = No

Finally, you must be very careful about the information you pass over the air, as radio traffic is often intercepted – sometimes by accident, and at other times by design. Either way, you can easily give your position and objective away without realising it.

When my team is working in a well-known area, each of the operators has a street map which is broken into sectors. Each sector has a code name, and streets are also given a code. By doing this, we all know where we are, and are not giving any information away that can be used to locate our positions or our objective. It is not always possible to pre-plan in this way, but keep it in mind so that when the opportunity arises you will be working as a professional. Obviously, names and addresses should never be communicated. If it is important to give this kind of information, go Ten Eight and use your mobile phone or a secure land-line telephone.

In some circumstances, the surveillance team may have to use covert radio communication systems. This type of equipment is usually used in close surveillance operations, such as when following a suspect. The equipment is discreetly secured to the operator, and can be voice-activated. The tiny microphone sits below the shirt neckline over the area of the voice-box. The listening device is also very tiny and fits snugly into the ear. Some have a hard wire attachment, while others need no wires but can be larger, and therefore more susceptible to discovery.

On occasions, there will be a need to follow or locate a vehicle. Following a vehicle visually is a relatively straightforward task, but location is a different matter and can take a great deal of time and manpower.

A more productive way is to use an electronic tracking system. This is a high-powered system designed to be user-friendly. Top-of-the-range models use satellite tracking and are extremely accurate, while the lower end of the spectrum also offers some very acceptable systems. These use magnetically mounted transmitters powered by internal batteries, and can be fitted to a vehicle in seconds. Once in place, the transmitter radiates a signal, which is picked up by a

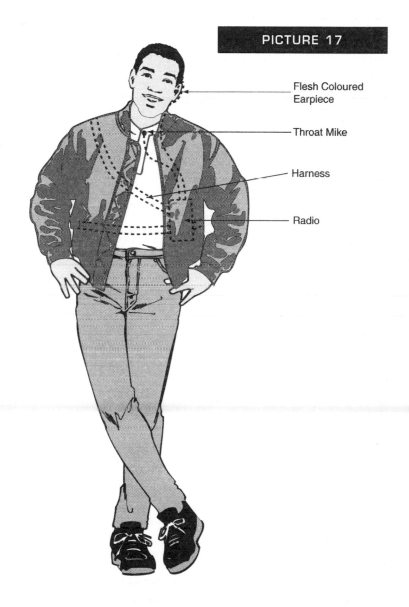

PICTURE 17

Flesh Coloured
Earpiece

Throat Mike

Harness

Radio

*On some operations the P.I. will carry
covert radio equipment*

receiver. The receiver is mounted in the surveillance vehicle and shows the received signal as an LED display, covering 360 degrees. The distance between the transmitter and receiver is also displayed by using a simple signal-strength meter. An added feature is audio output, which allows you to orientate by the change in sound signal – a very important feature when you are driving through traffic and can't take your eyes off the road.

Once you have the target vehicle in sight, it helps if you can video-record the event. Fitting a video camera and recording equipment in your vehicle is an easy procedure. The better the camera, the more versatile it will be in changing conditions and lighting levels. Using auto-iris equipment is the best way of ensuring that you get decent recordings. Fitted into a vehicle, the recording system will inevitably be shaken around and will need to be regularly checked and serviced.

Clothing

What to wear, and when, can be one of the most difficult problems the undercover operator has to overcome.

At all times, I carry an selection of alternative clothing in the boot of my car. For my day-to-day work, I generally wear a dark suit fitted with plenty of pockets. However, the wearing of formal dress isn't always a practical option, as on occasions at a moment's notice I have had to scale a wall, and make my way through dense foliage to gain an advantage. At other times, I have had to abandon my vehicle and catch trains, boats or planes in pursuit of my quarry.

Obviously, you haven't always got time to change your clothes, but you can easily change your appearance by carrying a newspaper or shopping bag. Taking your tie off, carrying your jacket over your arm or putting it in a shopping bag will also help. Carrying a change of footwear in your vehicle will also allow you to alter your appearance.

When choosing what to wear, the bottom line is to choose clothing that is discreet. As an investigator, you need to become a 'grey person' – the kind of person whom no-one notices. If you are anticipating working on an undercover operation, take time to visit the location area and take notice of the local dress. Look at the overall environment; choose several people of your own age and gender. Study their dress, the newspapers they read, the type of lunch-box they use, what type of vehicle they drive, etc. It is often worthwhile visiting local second-hand clothing shops in the area of operation, as the clothing sold there will reflect the local tastes. No matter where you are operating, ensure that you dress and act appropriately.

Remember, the rule is that you should be the one observing, not the one being observed. Develop the 'grey-man' approach!

PRACTICE SESSION

Choose a crowded room in a place where you are not known; this may be a bar or waiting room.

Practice entering without making your presence noticed.

Remember to avoid eye contact, but still pick out individuals who do not blend in easily.

Try to work out what it was that drew your attention to them.

After ten minutes or so, look around and find someone you have not noticed before. Watch them and try to work out what it was about them that caused you not to notice them.

Continue to carry out this exercise until you feel that you have started to develop the 'grey-man' ideals.

The target

The word 'target' is the term used to indicate the person or place that is the focus of an investigation.

Before taking on any investigation, make sure that you have a proper briefing and that all targets are properly identified. Likewise, make sure that the target is a legitimate one. There is no excuse for you being involved in tracing a target for a client who is the subject of a restraining order, or some other legal or moral reason why the client should not know the whereabouts of the target. Before taking on any job, insist on a face-to-face meeting with your client. Ask them their reasons for wanting the information or for locating the target, and ask them what they are going to do with the information that you supply. Be sure that you are properly briefed, and that you are not being asked to break any laws.

In the past, I have been asked to locate an adopted child for its natural mother, and vice versa. You should be aware that if you do locate the missing family member, they might not wish to be confronted by an estranged parent or child.

Once you are satisfied with the validity of your task, it's time to get down to planning your approach and setting the tasks.

Location

Before you can decide on the best method of investigation, you need to know the location and environment in which you will be working. Is it a warehouse, a factory, a bar or store? Will you have to follow someone? Do they drive, use a motorcycle, take the tram, a cab or walk? Are they located in a city, town, suburb or a mixture of them all? There is no substitute for pre-operation intelligence.

Identification

Sometime ago, I had a team of four operators placed in a shopping area in a quaint Surrey town in Great Britain. Unfortunately, our client didn't have a photograph of the target, although we did have a detailed description of him – even down to the clothes he was wearing. He was part of a seven-man team operating around the shopping area, stopping passers-by and engaging them in conversation in an effort to sell them security alarms.

Within an hour we had located the target; the description was as close as an eyelid to an eye. For the rest of the day we kept him under surveillance, relaying his every movement to our client. We even told her the make of his shoes, which she already knew and confirmed. During the late evening, I received a call from the client, thanking me for the day's surveillance. 'You know,' she said, 'I've just been speaking to him over dinner, and it was obvious he had no idea he'd been followed.' The problem was that we still had the guy under surveillance, and he wasn't anywhere near our client's home!

Up-to-date photographs, or access to someone who can properly identify the target for you, will save you a great deal of time and embarrassment. Even with a photograph, it is sometimes hard to positively identify a target. Other features such as mannerisms and tattoos all help.

On another occasion, I was in a covert observation position watching a group of young adult males. The observations were put in place to locate known terrorists. I had photographs of suspects, but other than being around the same age, there was no-one in the group that fitted them.

One guy in particular caught my eye. He was continually chewing and opening his mouth quite wide in an unusual way. I remembered reading a colleague's description of a guy who was suspected of planting a terrorist bomb. One of the features in the report was this unusual chewing style. I had a photograph of the suspect, but he had long hair and a bushy moustache. The guy I was looking at was clean-shaven with very close-cut hair.

The more I observed him, the more I thought he was the terrorist. Luckily, I was in radio contact with the operator who knew him. When I contacted him, he said the guy looked like a young John Lennon. Bingo! That description confirmed my suspicions, and opened up the surveillance to a point where the terrorist was kept under close surveillance and eventually arrested.

Look-alike descriptions are the best and most effective way of describing someone and remembering a person. Using well-known celebrities, politicians, etc. will enable you to quickly put a suspect into a specific human grouping.

Movement

The way in which people move around their environment can be put into broad categories. Some people stay very much in their local area, while others reside in one area and work in another some miles away. Many people are home for the weekend, but work and live away on weekdays.

People are basically creatures of habit. The way in which they walk, drive their cars, etc. doesn't change a great deal. Visiting the local shop, bar or community group at specific times and at specific places is all part of a person's movement through his environment. All these aspects of a person's life are very important to the investigator. Knowing how, when and why people move around will help to maintain a grip on surveillance and its planning.

The cautious target

In the main, people are not very surveillance-conscious and can be followed quite easily. However, once they do become surveillance-conscious, they are very difficult to follow successfully.

Some people lead the type of life that warrants close observation by the authorities. As a result, such people are very cautious and live their lives constantly expecting to become the subject of a surveillance operation. Carrying out surveillance on cautious targets requires a great deal of preparation and a very experienced team. They will constantly be looking over their shoulders, changing their direction time after time, going through red traffic lights, turning into cul-de-sacs and even having a buddy following in the background – all in an effort to shake off and pinpoint any surveillance operators. Many cautious targets will also employ closed-circuit television and electronic detectors around their properties, making pre-operation reconnaissance extremely difficult.

Even with all these factors working against a surveillance operation, it is still possible to undertake surveillance and to achieve positive results. Proper planning, patience and professionalism give a quality team the edge.

In a surveillance operation, it is usual for operators to feel that they have been seen. Good operators have to get over this feeling if they are going to be effective in the profession. Putting this feeling aside allows the operator to monitor the target properly and quantify any real concerns, which should be based on quality judgements and changes in the target's normal habits.

Direct/Indirect approach

On some occasions, it is possible to make a direct approach to the target in order to get the information required. However, this should only be done with the express agreement of the client. If the direct approach is considered, then thought should be given to the questions that need to be answered and the most suitable way of asking them.

An indirect approach may be by way of questions asked of neighbours, friends and relatives. Once again, this should only be undertaken with the client's full agreement.

In both of the above, you must ensure that you ask the questions, and that you are not drawn into a question session about you, your work or the client.

Throughout these approaches, and in fact in all other aspects of the work, consider whether your actions are likely to lead to a threatening or violent encounter. If you are unsure, work on the basis that you are more likely to upset someone, and be ready for that eventuality. Knowing that you may upset someone does not mean that you should not carry on with the task; it merely ensures that you are keeping yourself aware and considering ways of averting trouble.

Care
and safety

Private investigation is undoubtedly a risky business. Investigators run a much greater risk of being caught up in a violent incident than most other professionals do. A number of investigators have lost their lives as a result of their work, while others have been severely injured by assailants and explosive devices.

Being able to look after yourself in combat is a very important and difficult skill. To practice it requires many hours of time against opponents who know martial-arts techniques. The problem with using violence as self-defence is that you risk becoming the victim – that's not to say that you shouldn't practice some form of martial art. My preference is Tai Kwon-do. I find that it has helped me to control situations that have gone past the stage of reason.

However, by far the best form of self-defence is being able to talk to and integrate with people. There have been many occasions when I have been in fear of my safety. In the vast majority of these incidents, I have managed to control the situation by being professional and assertive. Assertiveness is a behaviour you can acquire, and I would encourage everyone employed in the business of investigation to take the time to train and develop this very important skill.

Before you go out on an investigation, make sure that all of your equipment is working properly – especially your communications equipment. Wherever possible, ensure that a second operator is working with you. Before leaving the office, make sure that you leave written details about the operation, where you are likely to be and your estimated time of arrival back at the office. If you have a manned office, call in at agreed times, just to let them know that you are OK. If your office isn't manned, call your answerphone and leave details on it. By doing this, if you have not returned home or made an agreed meeting, the police could use the information to retrace your steps.

A part of pre-operation planning should be risk assessment. Having taken the time to look at the risks, make sure that you have agreed emergency and safety procedures, and that all your colleagues are aware of them.

On one occasion, my team was tasked to occupy empty properties in an undercover observation. During the pre-operation planning, the local fire officer told us that there had been a number of incidents in which empty properties had been subject to firebomb attacks. As a result of this information, we trained for the eventuality and took fire extinguishers and fire blankets with us. In fact, we now take small individual fire extinguishers on all our static surveillance operations.

The mobile telephone is a great aid to safety. By keeping it constantly charged and close to hand, you can quickly summon help. If possible, have the police emergency telephone number programmed and ready to access at the touch of the Send button. Call it, even if you are not in a position to be able to speak properly to the operator. If you are in danger, then the operator will be able to hear what is going on and act accordingly.

It is also worth considering carrying a personal alarm, although obviously this may prove difficult in an undercover role. If you do carry one, keep it on you at all times. Stowing it at the bottom of luggage, as some people tend to do, renders it useless. If the attacker is close to you, make sure that you press the alarm against his ear, as the sound will disorientate him long enough for you to run away. If you are not able to use an alarm in this way, you can pretend to vomit – which will cause the attacker to move away, giving you the opportunity to run.

Occasionally, dogs may confront you. A dog dazer can help if you are quick enough to get one out and use it, but if not, it is down to you and the dog. Whatever you do, don't run – the dog will win! Stand still and face the dog, and remain as calm as possible, dogs can sense fear, and this gives them courage. Do not make sudden movements or wave your arms around. Likewise, do not kick out. Keep facing the dog, but avoid eye contact with it. Keep your eyes on its back, not on its head; this will lessen the chances of you inadvertently looking directly into its eyes, which might incite it to attack.

As the situation calms, back away slowly. If it does attack, use your dog dazer or fight it off with anything you can bring to hand, such as a stick, brick, luggage or anything else you can find. Hitting it hard in the throat or, better still, between the top of the chest and the base of the throat will stop it. A clenched fist brought powerfully down on top of the area between the base of the skull and the neck will render it unconscious.

Everyone involved at the sharp end of the investigation business should have up-to-date inoculations for all blood-borne diseases such as rabies.

Wearing protective clothing, such as stab- and bullet-proof vests, is worth considering if you are working in the type of environments in which you might need it, and with the kind of people who are likely to carry knives or guns.

When you are in a room, make sure that you are between the person and the door so that you can get out of the room quickly if need be. Keep your vehicle as close to you as possible, and parked in a position that enables you to leave the area quickly and easily – not facing into a dead-end, or parked above the property causing you to have to go past it to get away. When in a vehicle, keep the doors locked. In traffic, keep well back from other vehicles – at least one-and-a-half car lengths, so that you have the room to manoeuvre and get away in an emergency. Placing a simple pyrotechnic device, such as a blank shotgun cartridge or a theatrical maroon, under the driver's side of the vehicle that can be activated from within by a switch will give you an element of surprise and shock any assailant, giving you vital seconds to effect your escape.

It is also important for you and your colleagues to be qualified in first aid, and to carry a comprehensive first-aid kit in your vehicles.

Unfortunately, all the planning in the world cannot guarantee that you will not become a victim of violence. Work on the basis that you are likely to be a victim, and you will probably keep out of trouble.

If it does happen, then try to get away from it and put an obstacle between you and your attacker – a door, desk, vehicle, or whatever. If this proves impossible and you are confronted, try to back into a wall. Keep your eyes on the attacker's eyes at all times. Turn your body slightly so that you are presenting your shoulder, then lift the shoulder and tuck your head behind it. Keep your mouth shut and your forehead pointed at the attacker. By doing this, you will present less of a target for them to hit. Keeping your mouth shut will avoid a broken jaw if you are hit.

Place your feet firmly on the ground, pointing one foot at the attacker and keeping the lead knee slightly bent. Open the legs approximately eighteen inches to two feet apart, placing the rear foot across the front foot to form a 'T'. Keep the leg straight, to act as a stabiliser. Place your leading shoulder upper arm close to the breast, and the lower arm with fist clenched crossing the chest. Keep the rear arm extended with the fingers outstretched ready to counter a kick to the groin. Be ready to fend off the initial attack and in a position to counter it and to immobilise your attacker.

Violence is not usually a fair and equal exchange with the balance often upset by the use of a weapon. Countering attacks from weapon-carrying attackers is not easy, but is possible. The overriding factor is to keep calm and to control the action.

Knives and broken bottles are the most common form of weapons used in attacks, and handling attacks in which they are used requires very similar skills. Both weapons can inflict severe injuries. They are usually used in a stabbing, swinging or chopping motion, and the way in which the weapon is gripped will determine how it is going to be used. If a weapon is held in the clenched hand and protrudes from the thumb side, this indicates either a stabbing or swinging action. A weapon protruding from the little-finger side indicates that the weapon will be used in a high downward motion, as if chopping. Taking up the basic stance described earlier and wrapping a jacket or something similar around the leading forearm will allow you to ward off the initial strike. Thereafter you should work to push the attacker back and off balance, until you can overpower him. Using a chair with the legs pointed towards the face of the attacker and rushing forward, hitting him hard, will also have the desired effect.

Baseball bats and long axe-handles are sometimes used in violent attacks. These will be used in a swinging or clubbing action. Because they are long and have to be swung with an outstretched arm, the attacker can hit you from around four to five feet away. Clearly, being at the end of the swing is where the most damage can be caused. If you can't keep out of reach, go in close. Keeping within the sweep of the swing lessens the chance of being hurt. If you do get in that close, jab your fingers deeply into the attacker's eyes, or sharply slap both of his ears at the same time.

The same applies to attackers who carry long-barrelled guns such as a shotgun or rifle. These weapons become ineffective if you are very close to the attacker. Pistols, on the other hand, are designed to be used at close range. The essence of disarming an attacker with a pistol is firstly to divert it away from your body and then to dislodge it from the attacker's grip, while keeping it pointing away from you – a very difficult manoeuvre, but not an impossible one. Probably the best way is to hit the wrist sharply just above the hand holding the weapon. Grip the wrist and use your other hand to twist the weapon from the attacker's grip. Forcefully pushing your forehead into the face of the attacker will put him off balance.

Although it is not a regular occurrence, investigators may well be subjected to detainment either for short or long periods, especially when involved in industrial-espionage missions in other countries around the world. I have been detained at Nairobi Airport in Kenya, West Africa, by an over-enthusiastic customs officer who was of the opinion that I had been involved in some form of spy mission. It took me several hours and a bottle of whiskey before I managed to convince him of my innocence and carry on with my journey. On another occasion, I was arrested in Albania and had to pay a large 'fine' to the local police chief and his family.

Being bound with rope is one way of restricting you if you are detained. However, escape from this is not impossible, although you will have to decide whether or not an escape attempt is in your best interests. In any event, you should use recognised techniques to undermine the tying-up process so that should you wish to effect an escape you can discard the bindings.

The way you do this is to present parts of your body to be bound in such a way that the binding can be loosened afterwards. Present your hands in front of your body by keeping the heels of your hands together and slightly cupping them. At the same time, keep your hands close to your body with your elbows pushed out. This action causes your wrists to part. Binding you in this position allows you to straighten your arms, which will push your wrists together, thus loosening the bindings. Flattening your hands, palm to palm, will further loosen them until you can wriggle free. If a mouth gag is being used, push your chin on to your chest and puff your cheeks out. If at all possible, keep your teeth tightly closed. These positions will again allow you to loosen your bindings when you draw your chin in and stretch your neck to its full extent.

If your hands are being tied behind your back, present them thumb to thumb with your palms facing outwards and your arms slightly bent. Once again, try to ensure that there is a good gap between your wrists. Turning your hands palm to palm and drawing them up your back will loosen the binding and allow you to slip out.

If you are unfortunate enough to be illegally detained, it is vital that you quickly assess the situation. This is particularly true if you are the captive of a political or religious group. Although you may not think that you could be subjected to this type of event, I can tell you that over the years I have been involved in several investigations that have involved extremists from both of these categories. Generally, you will be told the reason for your detainment, but this is not always the case, and some groups deliberately do not tell you in order to use it as a powerful tool against you. Obviously, the chances are that you will not hold the same beliefs or be of the same nationality as the person or group who has detained you.

Given this fact, it is likely that you are going to be subjected to a harsh, if not violent regime. If you are one of a number of captives, then you should keep out of any disputes: the concept of being the grey man is very important in this type of situation. Blending in the background and posing no threat whatsoever will lessen the chances of you becoming a victim should detention deteriorate into violence. Adopting a very low profile in a group detention will inevitably lead to another detainee (who is unaware of the best action to take) becoming the focus of the aggressors. Sad though that is, you would be well advised to allow that to continue without your intervention, because if the situation becomes violent then it is more likely that a higher-profile detainee will be the one who is subjected to it.

Obviously, it is difficult not to react when you are being treated in a violent or uncomfortable manner, but as a professional you should look at the wider picture and consider that you may well be able to assist later in the arrest and conviction of your captors and your safe return. If you are detained, the very least you can expect is that you will be told to sit with your hands on your head. This may seem quite civilised, but in fact it is painful and uncomfortable to sit in this position for long periods without being able to move. No matter how uncomfortable it becomes, do not complain as complaining will single you out! In a group, someone less knowledgeable will probably complain, which will either fall on a sympathetic ear or will serve to begin the selection process of the first person singled out as the victim of violence.

As I have explained, bindings are uncomfortable, but they can be loosened. At the very least, flex your muscles and expand your limbs while you are being tied up. Once the ordeal is over, you can relax a little, allowing the bindings to loosen and your circulation to flow. Unfortunately, the situation may deteriorate to the point where you are subjected to a beating. In such a case, there is not a great deal you can do other than to take it as well you can. Keeping your arms close to your sides and chest will go some way to protect your body. Tucking your chin in and keeping your teeth tightly closed will lessen the injuries. To resist in some way will only make matters worse.

You may consider fighting back. However, if there is no chance of gaining an advantage, then don't try it. On another day, there may well be a chance. The best way of surviving is to show pain when it hurts. However, showing too much pain too soon will frustrate the aggressor, who will become impatient and harder in his approach. A display of arrogance by acting hard may look good in the movies, but doesn't work in real life. It may well even lead to your being beaten to death!

Many investigators, especially those with former law-enforcement or military backgrounds, have what is best described as a military bearing. They walk and act in a way that singles them out. As a professional investigator, you should be able to fit into any situation without being singled out. That is not to say that you should slouch around with a seemingly unconcerned attitude, as this will also bring attention on to you. An area that is very difficult to conceal is your non-verbal communication. As an investigator, you will develop a sense of awareness and an ability to pick up on other people's actions. Your eyes and facial expressions can register that you are listening, looking and taking in information. As a captive, these are the last things you want your captors to become aware of. It will be difficult for you to address this problem, as showing too little concern is as wrong as showing too much. Showing compassion for your captors can be as provocative as showing your hatred of them.

By far the best way of dealing with this situation is not to make eye contact with your captors. That does not mean that you should continually look away from them, as that will be met with disapproval. If you are forced to look straight at your captor, then do so – to cast your gaze elsewhere will be read as a defiant gesture. The chances are that you will not know when or if you are to be released, and it may be the case that your release will have to be secured by diplomatic negotiation. This will take time and you should prepare yourself for a long wait.

One way of combating the uncertainty and fear is to use your mental ability. Constructing something in your mind, such as a luxury home or grand garden – brick by brick or shovel by shovel – will help you to come to terms with your predicament. To brood is soul-destroying, and takes away your inner strength. Throughout your encounter, never forget that you are an investigator. Use all of your skills to find out everything you can about the situation and your captors. Keep a mental log of everything and everyone, but remember to remain the grey man. Once you are free, the information you have gained will probably be of use to your client, the police or your government.

The chances are that your survival will depend on keeping a low profile. Unfortunately, in some cases this type of professional approach may mean that others around you have been injured or even killed. You will feel that you should have intervened and done something to put an end to it. You may have regrets about your fear and the way you handled it. The truth of the matter is that in these unusual circumstances your instinct is to survive. The problem is that life does not teach us the reality of encounters such as these. As an investigator, you may well be put into a position that very few people have ever encountered. Investigation can be a very tricky, dangerous business. As an investigator, you will have to be able to cope with many unusual, frightening and potentially aggressive situations. It is this uncertainty and the way in which you deal with it that makes private investigation so attractive.

Exercise and culture plan

For quite a lot of the time, you will be sitting around or lying in surveillance mode for many hours, hardly daring to move. This lack of physical activity can be quite damaging to your general health. Regular physical exercise not only keeps you fit and healthy but also improves your mental ability as well. You may already keep a physical fitness routine; if so, make sure you keep it up. During the rigours of PI work, it is sometimes difficult to find time for yourself Obviously, if you are taking martial-arts classes, much of the fitness and stamina you need will already be in hand. In any event, you should have a daily exercise plan that can be carried out quickly and at all times during the day. Unfortunately, due to the unpredictable nature of the work, you will not be able to put a definite time aside every day, and you may have to fit your exercises in when and where you can. Nevertheless, you can keep an exercise maintenance programme going that can be completed without equipment within 20 minutes a day.

Over the years, I have been subjected to a number of physical-fitness regimes, especially during my time in the Army and within law-enforcement and close-protection roles in which I have been involved. I have used my experience as a personal trainer with individuals and teams who have gone on to undertake arduous tasks and expeditions in some of the most remote and dangerous parts of the world.

Without doubt, the single most important factor in personal fitness is the mind. If you do not have the right mental attitude, then any fitness regime will undoubtedly fail. Physical fitness is not achieved solely by exercise, and is not a matter of building muscles – it is a state of being. Without a healthy lifestyle and positive mind set, any exercise plan you do take part in will not be as beneficial as it could be. Well-being is achieved by developing your stamina and endurance.

In order to develop these vital areas, you need to concentrate your work on your heart and blood vessels. Known as the cardiovascular system, this is the way in which oxygen is transported around your body. The more oxygen you can get to your vital organs and muscle groups, the better you will feel. Improving this will not only improve your physical fitness, it will also greatly improve your ability to cope with stress, and a very important part of the investigator's life is being able to cope when under pressure. The power of the human brain is enormous, but it relies on a continual supply of oxygen. Its functions are improved when that oxygen is delivered unhindered by poor circulation.

As you exercise to improve the cardiovascular system, the rest of your body benefits. Your muscles will tone, and your fat levels will reduce. Once this happens, you will find that you will have increased ability in many physical areas, such as your overall flexibility and agility. You will become stronger, and have a great deal more explosive power and overall balance.

Before starting any fitness training, you should carry out a fitness evaluation. By doing this, you will be able to monitor your progress. Measuring your progress not only confirms that you are improving, but it can also help to keep you motivated. There are two simple tests that you can carry out before you start your training that will give you an idea of your current fitness. The first is a simple, yet effective, way of determining your current heart and lung fitness:

- Take a five-minute sit-down rest. During this time, keep as still as possible
- Now do a series of step-ups in quick succession for a timed one minute (this should be carried out by stepping up and down on a bench, secure chair or step with a height of approximately 15 inches. The bent leg should be straightened fully on the step up)
- At the end of the exercise, stand still and take a normal breath, and hold it for as long as you can without straining (do not take a big breath)
- You should be able to hold the breath for at least 30 seconds. Being unable to achieve this is a good indication that your fitness level is quite low

Another similar test I used in the military is the pulse-recovery test. Before trying this, refrain from eating, smoking or drinking for at least three hours:

- Once again, take a five-minute complete rest
- Before starting the exercise, take your resting pulse (this is known as your basic metabolic rate)
- Do step-ups as explained earlier for a full three minutes
- Now time how long it takes for your pulse to return to normal
- Keep a record of this, and use it to check your improvement after carrying out a regular fitness routine for several weeks

I would suggest that before you begin any fitness training, you should consult your doctor and undergo a thorough medical examination. Even when you are fit and training regularly, you should have regular medical and dental checks. Doing this will not only underpin your training, but will also ensure that you are fit enough to go anywhere in the world at a moment's notice. Investigating is a demanding business, but it will be much more difficult if you are so unfit that you are puffing and panting or in pain from a severe toothache.

In my opinion, the best exercise anyone can take is walking. It costs nothing to do, can be undertaken virtually anywhere and exercises the whole body. The problem is that it takes a lot of time. If you do find the time, then you should use it to power walk. Power walking is a very effective exercise. Choose a flat route and start the walk briskly. After half a mile walk as fast as you can stretching your legs to a full but comfortable stride and swinging your arms to keep a good balance. Keep this pace going and try to extend the walk to take in a hill or two. You should begin with a two- or three-mile walk, extending this to 10 or 15 miles. Do the power walking as part of the following routine: walking a two- to three-mile route weekly with a ten- to fifteen-mile route at least once a month, although if you can fit it in more times then do so, as it will only do you good.

If it is difficult to put this amount of time aside each week, make a point of walking as much as you can during the working day. You can do this by parking your vehicle further away from your meeting places than you would normally do. Taking the stairs instead of the lift will also help to develop a healthy cardiovascular system.

As I have already indicated, in today's society our bodies and minds are often forced into a passive existence that is not conducive to good health or an active mind. As investigators, the majority of us spend more time sitting or lying down than we do engaged in some form of physical exercise.

All too often, we hear of a friend or colleague suffering a heart attack after some mild form of physical stress. Many of us sit out the winter months, and at the first sight of spring we go out into the garden and find that we are out of puff after a couple of lifts of the spade or the lifting of a bag of compost. Once we are aware of the lack of fitness, we decide to do something about it, such as taking up a sport or finding a local gym, but after only a few weeks we give it up and revert to our passive mode of life.

If there is one thing worse than no exercise, it's spasmodic exercising; it does you no good, and can in fact be fatal! Exercising is not just a physical effort; it requires a mental effort and a philosophical outlook. The following plan encompasses both aspects, and is designed as an ongoing process, which will fit the busy investigator's lifestyle.

The plan

WARNING

Do not attempt the exercises without first reading the guidelines below.

Keeping healthy

First of all, prior to any exercising you should consult your doctor and ask him for his advice about your overall condition, and whether or not he thinks you are able to cope with the exercising you are about to undertake.

It is important that you keep to the number of exercises I give you, even though you feel you can do more. The system is designed to build you up steadily and with natural progression. If you miss one day's exercise, then you must do two extra days; if you miss more than two days, then you must go back to the very beginning – no matter how far on you are, it is important that you complete the two-week programme without interruption.

The basic psychology

In this programme of exercise, you can monitor your progress by results; however, to get results, you first have to have effort. Throughout, you need to strive to become as successful and sharp as you can – both physically and mentally. Strive to focus your mind, maintain your inner courage and fear nothing, have absolute confidence in your ability, develop the power of will by faith and persistence; the truest success is the development of self. Always think health, radiant health; rise above your negative impulses, make each exercise count; think power, strength and tone into every movement.

Where possible, practice your exercises in the nude in front of a full-length mirror. Do the exercises with poise and grace, and above all remember that spasmodic effort will get you nowhere. Exercising is mainly a product of habit, and once you get into it, your day will be incomplete without it. You must cultivate good habits and destroy bad ones. Kicking bad habits is hard, but the person who truly wishes to conquer them may destroy all habits.

As you exercise, look at yourself in the mirror. Be conscious of each movement, and remember to think strength and power. Concentrate on your heart, blood vessels and lungs, and avoid all half-hearted effort. As you exercise, you will be getting rid of poisonous, dead tissue, which will be replaced by new tissue which will give you longevity and elasticity.

Before exercising, prepare your mind and body for the task. Warm up by standing with your feet together, arms stretched out in front of you at shoulder level; keep your back straight, point your fingers and now force your arms forward above your head, stretching to touch the ceiling, then to your left and then to the right, stretching all the way. Standing with your back to the wall and about 15 inches away, slowly touch your knees with the palms of your hands, then stretch your arms over your head and touch the wall behind you with your fingertips. Once you have stretched, stand by an open window or door and take several deep breaths; aim to fill your lungs with pure air, but do not strain. You can practice the deep breathing as often as you like throughout the day.

Personal development

Make every effort to correct your posture; always sit upright, walk upright, look the world in the eye and look alive at all times. Throughout the day, stretch to the ceiling, and constantly review your reasons for health and fitness. Be the master of your own will. Take pride in your appearance, and choose friends with clean mental and physical outlooks.

Avoid brooding and worry, and constantly think power and success. Substitute negative thoughts with thoughts of health, power and courage. Eliminate fear. Physical health is a mental tonic; encourage rhythm, grace and poise. Develop strength of character; eliminate spasmodic, angular movements. Turn aside from anger and annoyance. Be a larger, nobler self; think high and powerful thoughts. Listen to no idle talk and avoid mental waste; keep your own counsel.

Storing and increasing energy

Sleep is the universal rejuvenation of the mind and body. Where possible, get to bed before 10pm – two hours before midnight is better than four hours afterwards. I know this is difficult when you are an investigator, but wherever possible take advantage and get to bed. There will be times when you will not be able to get a good night's sleep, and other times when you will have to use all of your stored inner strength to combat fatigue.

When you do have the opportunity to follow the rejuvenation sleep, make sure you secure undisturbed sleep, by sprawling out in your bed. Consciously rest your body, starting with your face, neck and shoulders; slowly rest your torso and limbs, and hold thoughts of your future health and success. Avoid tense, stiff muscles. Go to bed to sleep, to gather fresh strength. Saturate the mind with pleasant thoughts. Keep your room tidy and pleasant with a temperature around 50–70 degrees F. Use a hard mattress and a light pillow. Keep a window open and breathe deep fresh air.

In the morning, do not lie in bed; get up straight away, stand by the open window, and take deep slow breaths. Take a drink of warm water with a little lemon or honey before doing anything else. Use very cold water to wash in, and bathe the solar plexus and groin with water as cold as you can stand; dry these areas vigorously with a rough towel until you feel a warm glow.

Hygiene

When warm, for example after exercising, take a cool shower (not cold), or rub the body with a cool face-cloth, wipe the excess water away with the bare hand and finish with a Turkish, towel down, and dress while still warm. At least twice a week, take a bath in warm water – too hot, and you will lose your strength. Use good-quality soap, starting with your feet, and move towards the heart in an effort to push the blood back through the veins. At least once a week, strip off your clothing and allow your body to breathe. Let the air circulate around, and after an hour apply olive oil to your skin, smoothing the muscles from your feet towards the heart, and massage your scalp with olive oil. When your work allows, take a bath before going to bed.

In surveillance operations, there will be times when you will be eating, sleeping and having to go to the toilet using a plastic bag while in close proximity to your team members. Believe me, you will soon know who your friends are in these close-quarter operations. Make sure that you keep yourself as clean and tidy as possible. This is not just for your sake, it is also for the sake of the rest of the team. Personal hygiene is a very important part of professional investigation, and should not be overlooked.

Keeping yourself clean in covert surveillance operations is not easy, and requires some explanation. Obviously, water is at a premium, as in most cases you will not be in a position to use water from taps. However, you should keep a little aside for your ablutions. You will be surprised how little water you need to maintain a clean appearance. When you are putting together your covert kit, make sure you pack a 250ml plastic bottle of water, a small face-cloth and a tiny bar of odourless soap, toothbrush and small tube of paste.

After you have been in the covert observation position for some time, you will want to freshen yourself up. This not only keeps you clean, but also refreshes you so that you can continue to do your job with renewed sharpness. Whenever possible, put a little toothpaste on your brush and brush your teeth. Use your mouth saliva to wash your mouth out and spit it into a tissue. As with all your waste, you should take this with you by putting it into a separate bag that is used for all of your rubbish. Having done this, wet a corner of your face-cloth and rub it on to your bar of soap. Now wash your face with a series of small circular motions. Concentrate on the areas around your mouth, nose and ears. Now use the face-cloth in the same way to wash your hands, making sure you clean under your nails as you do this. You can remove the dirt from under your nails by scraping it out with a split match or other similar implement. Once you have completed this, wet another part of the face-cloth with clean water. Use this to clean around your eyes, before carrying on to remove the soap from the rest of your face and hands. On prolonged surveillance operations, you can use this method to wash the whole of your body. If you have to do this, start with the head and work down to your feet, making sure you wash your groin.

Diet

If you are grossly overweight, you must use a well-tested nutritional dietary plan that is designed personally for you, and which will help you to lose weight while giving you the vital vitamins needed to stay healthy. In essence, if you are training regularly you can virtually eat what you wish, as long as it adds up to a balanced diet, and you keep your food intake to a sensible level.

Wherever possible, avoid eating white bread, white flour products, all fatty meats, and excessive amounts of sharp spices, including salt – in any event, keep your salt intake to an absolute minimum. Commercial sweet products and white sugar should be avoided. Ordinary rice, spaghetti, macaroni, tea and coffee can be taken, but only in moderation. Allay thirst with pure cool water, sipping it slowly. As an investigator, your lifestyle will be such that you will have to rush or miss meals. Wherever you can, avoid eating a wholesome meal until you have the time to do it justice; take a light snack with a glass of skimmed milk until you have the time to eat properly. When you do have a substantial meal, do not drink too much fluid during it, or for at least half an hour before or after. Enjoy the meal in pleasant surroundings, and in a pleasant frame of mind take your time when eating, chewing your food slowly in an effort to mix the food in your mouth with saliva before swallowing.

When you are In a prolonged surveillance operation, make sure you take lots of clean water with you and a good supply of dried fruit. I have spent periods as long as 14 days in the attics of houses without the occupants even knowing I was there. In these conditions, personal hygiene and a well-balanced diet are essential.

Constipation

Travelling from country to country, missing meals and essential sleep, and living with the stress of the day-to-day problems of the private investigator will inevitably upset your body's normal routine. A way of keeping yourself in the best condition possible is to keep your intestines sweet and clear. Be sure that when you do get the chance to use the toilet properly you fully evacuate yourself at least once a day – waste can be absorbed through the intestines and enters the blood stream. Never put off the urge to use the toilet. Once there, make every effort to fully clear the bowels. The more water you drink, the easier it will be to go to the toilet.

If you do become constipated, which can happen a lot in the haphazard life of an investigator, use a little Agar Agar – a gelatinous carbohydrate obtained from seaweed and a natural medium for bacteria that acts as a laxative, or you can soak prunes overnight and drink the juice and chew the flesh.

Personal progress chart

Prior to starting the exercise plan, complete this section first.

	WEEK 1	WEEK 6	WEEK 12
WEIGHT			
WAIST			
HIPS			
CHEST			
THIGHS			
PULSE RATE			

While relaxing, take your pulse rate – i.e. the number of beats per minute. Step up on to a chair for one minute and retake your pulse, relax and take your pulse at five-minute intervals until it returns to normal.

	WEEK 1	WEEK 6	WEEK 12
RELAXED RATE			
AFTER STEP-UPS			
AFTER 2 MINUTES			
AFTER 5 MINUTES			
AFTER 6 MINUTES			

Exercise plan

ARM RAISES

Stand with your feet slightly apart and your arms by your side. Tilt your head as far back as possible and look up pointing your chin high – you should feel the front and sides of your neck being stretched. From this position, fully straighten your arms by pushing the heels of your hands down towards the floor and flatten your palms, straightening your fingers and pulling them back.

Keeping your arms straight, slowly lift them in an arc in front of your body, stopping when your arms and palms are pointing upwards. At the same time lift your right leg, bending the knee to keep the sole of the foot at a right-angle to the floor. Hold this position when the thigh is level with the hip, finally pointing your right toes down as far as they will go. Reverse the procedure slowly until you return to the start position. Repeat the exercise, lifting your left leg. When you return to the start position, this is count one.

POWER PRESS-UPS

Place two chairs in front of you with a space between them large enough for your chest to pass through. Place the palms of your hands on the chairs, keeping your arms straight and locked at the elbows. Now straighten your body and legs out stretched behind you, taking the weight on your toes. From this position, you should be looking through the gap in the chairs to the floor. Keeping your palms flat on the chairs and your body rigid, slowly lower yourself through the gap by bending at the elbows until your chest is level with your hands. From this position, push up until you straighten your arms and lock your elbows. Count one.

(If you are not used to exercising and cannot carry out this exercise, you can build your upper-body strength by standing approximately four feet away from a wall, with your feet together. Facing the wall, put your arms out in front of you at shoulder height and width. Without moving your feet, lean forward, supporting your body weight by placing the palms of your hands on the wall and keeping your arms locked at the elbows. From this position, slowly bend your arms and lower yourself until your forehead touches the wall. From this position, push yourself away until your arms return to the locked position).

SIDE BENDS

Stand with your feet two to three feet apart, with your head, neck and back perfectly upright, and looking forward. Put your arms down by your sides with the palms flat and touching the outside of your legs, with the fingers together and pointing to the floor. Keeping your legs rigid and knees locked, slide your left hand down your leg, pushing it as far as it will go and then a little more, bending your body sideways without twisting. At the same time, lift your right arm straight out, keeping your fingers together and pointing out. As the arm reaches the position level with the shoulders, turn your palm to face up, unlock the elbow and bring your palm over as if to pat yourself on the head. Keep your fingers together, palm flat and pointing, and try to touch your left shoulder by forcing your forearm over the head as far as possible. Your upper arm should come into contact with the side of your head. Return to your start position and repeat the exercise on the other side. When you again return to the start position, count one.

DO NOT BEND BACK; DO NOT FORCE THE MOVEMENT

SQUATS

Stand upright with your feet apart at shoulder width. Place your hands on your hips, keeping your back perfectly straight ahead and the eyes looking forward. From this position, slowly lower yourself down by bending at the knees; keep your feet flat on the ground, and do not allow your heels to leave the floor. Keeping your back straight, sit as low as you can then slowly stand. When you return to your start position, count one. Do not rush!

BURPEES

Stand upright with your feet together and your arms stretched in the air, with your upper arms touching your ears and your flat palms facing forward with your fingertips stretching to touch the ceiling. Tilt your head back and look up. From this position, without moving your feet, bend your body and knees until your palms are flat on the floor either side of your knees, approximately shoulder-width apart. Keeping your palms flat, push up with your feet and force your legs back, until you are balanced on your toes, take your body weight on your locked straight arms and toes. Your body should be rigid and adopting the press-up start position. Lower your body down to a half-press-up position. When you reach that position, press up and at the same time bring your knees up to your chest and stand up. Count one. The whole of this movement should be flowing with no pauses, and carried out as quickly as possible.

SIT-UPS

Lie flat on your back with your hands clasped behind your head and elbows pointed out in line with your shoulders. Bend your knees a little and place your feet flat on the floor. Without pulling yourself forward with your hands, sit up and bend forward until your head comes into contact with your legs. Lower yourself back to the lying position. Count one. To obtain the greatest benefit from this exercise, you should carry it out slowly and powerfully. It may help if someone holds your feet down for you, or you can wedge your feet under a heavy chair. If you do not have the strength in your abdomen to carry out this exercise, you can build up your stomach muscles by doing the sit-ups while lying on a bed.

SPOT RUNNING

From a standing start, run on the spot, making sure your knees come up as far as they possibly can. At the same time, bend your arms and clench your fists very tightly. Adopt a normal running style with your arms, i.e. left arm moving with right leg, etc. Now exaggerate your arm movement so that you are forcing your elbows as far behind you as they will go. Count 20 paces as your left foot hits the ground. Stop and perform a half-squat, then stand upright. Count one.

Use these simple exercises to improve your overall fitness by following the following twelve-week plan:

	wk 1	wk 2	wk 3	wk 4	wk 5
ARMS RAISE	6	6	7	8	10
PRESS UPS	6	6	7	8	10
SIDE BENDS	6	8	10	12	14
BURPEES	2	5	6	8	10
SIT-UPS	5	8	10	12	14
SPOT RUNNING	2	3	4	4	5

wk6	wk7	wk8	wk9	wk10	wk11	wk12
15	15	20	20	24	26	30
15	15	20	20	25	25	30
16	20	20	30	35	35	40
12	16	16	18	20	25	30
18	20	20	25	25	30	35
5	8	8	10	15	20	25

TEST WEEK

Week 6 - Mark down the most you can do of each exercise.
Week 12 - Mark down your totals and beat your week-6 totals.

	WEEK 6	WEEK 12
ARMS RAISE		
PRESS UPS		
SIDE BENDS		
BURPEES		
SIT-UPS		
SPOT RUNNING		

PRACTICE SESSION

FIGHTING ART

Practice the fighting stance until you can go into it without thinking.

Practice the fighting techniques using a rolled-up newspaper to simulate a knife, bottle, rifle and pistol.

Practice being bound by your buddy until you can quickly effect a release from your bindings.

HYGIENE

Using a strong plastic bag, practice going to the toilet in a confined place. You may find this distasteful, but it is far better to practice this before you have to carry it out on a covert surveillance operation. You should practice until you can master it with the least amount of fuss.

Using a face-cloth and small bottle of water, practice washing yourself using the method explained earlier.

Introduction to industrial espionage

Industrial espionage can broadly be described as the illegal collection of information and data belonging to a person or company for use by another person or company without the permission of the owners. This definition covers a very wide field of activity, ranging from the operator who dresses as a tramp when systematically sifting through refuse bins to find and record discarded sensitive information, to the high-tech electronic engineer who accesses delicate and secret information by electronically tapping into a company's computer and communications network. Industrial espionage is a world-wide business that permeates all levels of society and commerce.

Industrial-espionage operators will use all manner of techniques to gain the upper hand, perhaps operating undercover with assumed names or bogus businesses, often under the guise of being business consultants, management advisers or executive analysts. These agents operate in a very professional manner, and are notoriously difficult to detect.

Their methods of operation are extremely varied, and can stretch from a simple search of a company file to strategically placed operators paid by a rival company to work undercover and gain the trust and confidence of top executives. These 'sleepers' can stay in location for many years, feeding information back to their handlers. On occasions, covert and undercover infiltration is not the answer, and other ways of gaining much-needed information are employed. Breaking into a company's premises – either as an undetected intruder or by making the entry look as though it has been perpetrated by local thieves – gives the industrial-espionage operator the opportunity to take photographs of sensitive documents, or access the company's computer system, copying customer lists, costing details, drawings, newly developed equipment, etc.

Clearly, the vast array of electronic bugging equipment discussed in

PICTURE 18

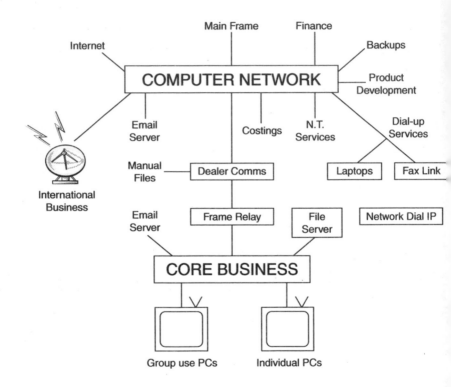

*Being able to hack into a businesses computer network
gives the Industrial Espionage operator
a great deal of information*

detail earlier in the book gives the industrial-espionage operator an enormous advantage over his prey. New and more sophisticated equipment is being developed virtually daily, and much of this has resulted from the needs of the industrial-espionage operator.

Industrial espionage is not solely a problem in multinational companies. Every firm, no matter how small, can be subjected to this type of activity. A large company may be looking to expand its activities or its sales base into another country or continent, and an easy way of doing this is to acquire a smaller company already working on similar products or with an existing foothold in another country. In such cases, the industrial-espionage operator can be called in to spy on the company in question, either to assist in determining its worth or to identify its weaknesses. This kind of information will be very useful when a buy-out offer is made, or in forcing an unwilling company to sell.

In some instances, the company under 'review' may be in the process of developing equipment for military use. Clearly, this information could be of interest to foreign governments, as well as business competitors. Industrial intelligence is an area of information that naturally attracts the attention of secret-service agents the world over. Consequently, it is likely that industrial-espionage operators may be recruited by foreign security services. Information gathering in this role may well be as simple as collecting company information and profiles from world trade fairs, or, at the other end of the scale, at the very top of international spying.

Being able to operate in foreign countries at a moment's notice is a pre-requisite for the industrial-espionage operator and the counter-espionage investigator.

Countering industrial espionage

C ountering the activities of industrial-espionage operators is the work of the private investigator, and is a very lucrative area for investigators who take on this type of work. Such investigators will employ many of the skills used by the industrial-espionage operator.

The most obvious is the use of electronic surveillance equipment. Countering industrial espionage should begin with an electronic de-bugging sweep of a company's key communication, sensitive development and boardroom areas. This should be carried out with the knowledge of the smallest number of people possible, and outside normal working hours, so as not to arouse suspicion. At the very least, use a modular-based multi-detection system covering RF detection, mains carrier, camera, infrared and live-wire detection.

If you do find a bug or series of bugs, you will then have to make the decision either to remove them, or to leave them in place and use them as a way of feeding false information, or monitoring them to locate the source.

Another sensible precaution is to use a facsimile monitoring system. These are multi-lined and enable you to monitor and record facsimile messages from a remote location. The intelligence gained from this equipment may well indicate the location or identity of the industrial-espionage operator. Once you have located the undercover operator, you can implement a system of electronic controls on all lines of communication within his work area, as well as an external surveillance operation based around his out-of-work life. This will eventually uncover who employs him. Once the industrial-espionage operator has been discovered, the client may wish to keep the rogue employee in employment and feed him with false information.

Computer investigation methods

C omputers can work both for and against an investigator. Obviously, the amount of information available at the press of a key makes the computer the greatest weapon in the investigator's armoury. However, the same can also be said for the criminal. The massive growth in information technology has led to an equally massive growth in criminal activity. From the relatively easy production of false identification documents, forgery and large-scale complex fraud to the hacker and paedophile, the computer offers a relatively safe method of exploitation.

If we assume that the industrial-espionage operator is a sleeper and therefore has easy access to a company's computers, his first obstacle will probably be to bypass any computer security, which in most cases involves the use of a password – the word used is often a family name, or some other word in everyday use. This can easily be carried out with the use of a dedicated CD that is designed as a code breaker, and runs through tens of thousands of words, names and combinations in a matter of minutes. The chances are that the password will be on the CD.

Another simple way for an industrial-espionage operator to find out a user's password is to watch the user as they log on to their computer system. This may be done over a number of days, marking down parts of the password each time they are observed. You will find that many computer operators use their family's names as the password. These are easily discovered by the astute industrial-espionage operator, who, noticing family photographs on the user's desk, asks who they are and what their names are!

One way of keeping the operator out is to change the password on a frequent basis, while another is to incorporate both letters and numbers in the password. Authorised computer users should be discouraged from incorporating any family names or dates of birth in their password.

There are times when an industrial-espionage operator cannot get into a position that allows him to operate in such an easy way. On occasions, I have been involved with operators who have rented an office overlooking the target's offices. From this remote location, the operator has set up a high-powered telescope and watched the target's staff entering the offices through a coded entry system. Within an hour, he has been able to record the sequence and later used it to gain unauthorised entry.

This method is often used to oversee a computer user's input from a remote location. In one particular investigation in which I was involved, the industrial-espionage operator set up a video camera, and at the end of each day he dispatched the film of the day's input to his handlers, who were able to use the information to undermine the legitimate company's pricing structure.

I am also aware of at least one instance in which a well-known bank had several customers complaining that their cash card had been stolen and used to obtain money from cash dispensers. The bank was adamant that the cards were either being used by their customers, who were acting illegally by having the cash themselves and claiming a loss, or they had kept their personal identification number with their card and both had been stolen. A great rift had developed between the bank and its customers, as the customers denied either being involved or breaching the bank's rule that cards and personal identification numbers must not be kept together. The clients blamed the bank, saying that there must have been some sort of collusion between the card thief and a bank employee, who gave the identification numbers to the thief. The bank was adamant that their computer system was such that no employee could access the information.

The ensuing investigation firstly indicated that all of the cards had been stolen on three consecutive days and from the same geographical area. A visit to the area revealed that the bank had a small branch within a mile of the thefts. The cash dispenser was located on an outside wall and overlooked by apartments. A cash dispenser transaction was re-enacted by an investigator, which showed that when in use, the finger dial could be seen from three apartments. A counter-industrial espionage surveillance operation was put in place with the brief to watch the apartments. Over the next two weeks, investigators noticed that in one of the apartments the occupant altered the position of the window-blind following certain cash-point transactions. Although this was an unusual event, the action appeared to have no real significance, as during the two weeks of surveillance, there were no incidents of cash being illegally obtained by cash-dispenser transactions or any cash cards being stolen.

Because of the unusual positioning of the window blind, it was decided that another week of surveillance should be carried out. During that week, the observer noted down several occasions on which the window-blind was re-positioned. Towards the end of the week, a report came in that a cash card had been stolen in the area and used to obtain money from another cash point. The investigators matched this with a particular day and then looked at the surveillance log. On the day in question, the blind had been moved on two occasions. The times of these occurrences were noted and one of them corresponded to the cardholder's legitimate withdrawal from the target cash dispenser.

The investigators then carried out a series of false transactions using several different investigators. Some of the transactions were carried out in such a way that allowed the finger pad to be seen from the apartment, and some in which the investigator positioned his body to shield the pad. On the ones with the pad in full view the blind moved as the investigator finished the transaction. Following this, another observation point was set up by the team in an empty apartment close to the one under suspicion. From this point, the observer could see more or less the same view as the blind-mover. After several transactions the blind moved, the bank surveillance team indicated this fact to the apartment team, who then carefully watched the action around the cash point and beyond.

For the first three transactions nothing seemed to be unusual – the observers saw a group of people going about their everyday lives. At the fourth attempt, it was noted that a young adult male who had been standing in a doorway near to the cash point moved and another young female took his position. This action became the focus of the apartment team's attention. Before long, it became clear that when a cash-dispenser customer stood in a position that allowed the finger-pad to be seen, the blind moved and one of the young adults in the doorway followed the customer.

The intelligence gained from this operation was passed to the local police, who confirmed that the young people involved were known pickpockets. A raid on the apartment by the police revealed a high-powered telescope trained on the cash-point finger-pad. The powerful equipment magnified the pad to a point whereby the four-digit personal identification number could easily be read. Once the operator was sure he had the number he moved the blind, indicating that fact to the watching pickpockets, who then followed the customer hoping that they could get them into a safe position to steal their card. When they had managed this, they handed the card to another member of the team who was waiting in a parked car. This 'runner' then drove to another cash dispenser and used the stolen card and personal identification number to fool the bank's computer into parting with as much cash as the customer's account would allow.

The only way to combat a remote operator using this type of technique is to ensure that computer monitors are turned to face into the office and not positioned in such a way that they can be read from a remote location. Likewise, ensure that any coded-entry system has a protective shield around it to minimise the chances of anyone being able to watch the code being input.

Another well-known and much-used method of infiltration is by computer hacking. The term is used to indicate an unauthorised method of gaining access to a computer or its network, either by using inside information or by hacking into the system by infiltrating the company's direct-dial communication line or via the Internet. The hacker will gain access to company information through the direct-dial route either by using a known employee's user identification or by building his own identification into the system. He can do this quite easily: either by co-opting someone on the inside to enter his undercover identification details for him; or alternatively by using someone else's security details and, once in the system, entering his own – allowing him unlimited access to the company's information. There are a number of people operating as computer hackers. Many of them are extremely effective hackers, and with each experience they become even more adept.

Generally, if a hacker has no inside help, he will have to hack into a system by multiple attempts until he can find a user name that allows him access to the client's private network. One way of combating hackers is to use software that allows only two or three attempts in accessing a system before shutting them out permanently.

A professional hacker can also access a company's computer system through the Internet – once again, the opening is created by finding a user identification that allows the hacker to cross from the Internet link to the intranet, the company's in-house version of the Internet. These sites are usually accessed by a number of legitimate users through a cluster of agreed Internet Protocol (IP) addresses. The hacker will begin by trying a variety of approaches until he locates a suitable and acceptable IP address. Once he has done this, he can bombard the site with a variety of possible user codes until he finds one that allows him access to all the company's information. Once inside, there is little chance of his presence being noticed.

One way of combating this type of access is by the use of a 'firewall'. As the name implies, this is designed as a barrier between the internal and external worlds. When properly set up, an Internet firewall is a very effective deterrent to the hacker.

Unfortunately, there is little that can be done when an industrial-espionage operator has access to, and uses, a legitimate operator's computer terminal. Unless there was any reason for suspicion, no-one would ever know that the computer was being used to supply information to an outside, unauthorised source.

An industrial-espionage operator operating in this way may not only use the computer to access information, but may also use it to create his reports. Even if this is not the case, the chances are that he will have regular (probably authorised) access to a personal computer in his undercover role. Although he may well write reports and use other programs to keep his handlers fully informed, then delete them from his computer, the chances are that he will not have completely removed them. For example, some programs are designed automatically to save work in a temporary file – often without the user's knowledge. This saved material can be located and viewed at a later date, even though the author did not save it in the normal way.

Even information that has been properly deleted can still be rescued. Imagine the hard drive of the computer as being a little like a human brain. Events and information that have been long forgotten are stored in the inner depths of the brain, yet it is still there in the deepest recesses, and its recall can be triggered by events or hypnosis.

The computer hard-drive's binary data is in the lowest levels of the computer brain. All information that has been input will have left a footprint. The operating system saves space by 'allocating' free space. Often this is virgin space that has not been used before. As you can imagine, there is a lot of used space that could be re-allocated and overwritten, but in fact has not been, and as such the 'deleted' information is still recorded there. Accessing this can be the key to uncovering an undercover industrial-espionage operator.

There are forensic computer investigators who specialise in the rescue of deleted or partially destroyed information stored within the depths of all computers, no matter how large or small.

Obviously, this kind of information can also be accessed by industrial-espionage operators, and can therefore theoretically be used by an unscrupulous company against a legitimate company. The military have developed programs that ensure that all the information deleted and held in the depths of the binary data is scrambled, and cannot be reorganised into the original text. Because of the massive financial investment by military and government security departments, similar programs are available for general use that can ensure, as far as possible, that deleted data is scrambled to the point where it can not be read.

Of course, information may have been removed from the computer to be stored on a floppy disk, CD or other storage medium. In some cases, this type of storage may have been destroyed, usually by breaking the component parts and, in the case of the floppy disk, actually cutting up the disk into small pieces. If you come across this situation in the course of your work as a private investigator, do not overlook or discard the damaged material, as in many cases you can reassemble the pieces like a jigsaw. In many cases, the 'lost' information will be recoverable – even after extensive damage has occurred.

During an investigation, be aware that you should not overlook or discard anything that may have some benefit. Even old computers that you find lying around in the office or storeroom may hold the key to a successful outcome to your investigation. The fact that they are in or around the premises suggests that they were probably used prior to an IT update. The unsuspecting hacker or industrial-espionage operator may well have left a footprint that will lead you directly to them.

As I have already indicated throughout this book, your work as a private investigator will be greatly enhanced if you tackle each new job with a common-sense approach, and you are able to motivate and discipline yourself and be ingenious in your thinking. Without doubt, when you start to investigate something such as computer fraud, all of these attributes will be needed. In most cases, you will be expected to work outside normal working hours, and probably over a weekend or public holiday. The benefit of working at these unsociable times is that you are less likely to be compromised by inquisitive members of the client's staff.

I am reminded of a recent investigation that involved a medium-sized company's computer network. Some of the computers were running CAD programs, and were all individually coded. As part of an investigation into fraud and theft, I needed to know who was doing what and when. Having been involved in this type of fact-finding mission before, I knew what to expect, as did my buddy, a computer expert. We began examining the first computer at 6.50pm on the

Friday, and worked straight through until 6a.m. on the Monday. We finished with just 30 minutes to spare before the first of the company's staff arrived. During the whole weekend, we managed to snatch just four hours' sleep.

Corporate fraud

Corporate fraud has increased dramatically, aided by the development of computers in the workplace. Corporate fraud is nothing more than theft of money. Put money and people together, and sooner or later you will have a theft. Add a computer to the equation, and you are likely to have a larger theft sooner. The problem with computer-aided fraud is that it tends to be quite sophisticated and well-hidden. In fact, most corporate fraud of this nature is discovered by accident. The use of regular routine investigations does help to uncover corporate fraud, and probably stops some potential fraudsters.

Basic fraud may involve altering sales figures to show a greater proportion of new clients by false invoicing, or showing an increase in orders so that the perpetrator can qualify for a sales bonus or extra commission. Another example of fraud is the inclusion of an extra member of staff on the payroll, the salary being paid by computer to a bogus bank account. Transferring large amounts of money to a personal high-interest account for short periods of time and returning it to the proper account before it is missed – and keeping the interest earned – is another common fraud. Another is the setting-up or use of an existing maintenance or hire company that forwards invoices for work carried out or for equipment hire when none has actually taken place – the account being overseen and signed off by the in-house fraudster. These are just a few simple examples of computer-aided fraud that demonstrate the need for investigators to be constantly employed by large organisations to stem the flow of financial crime.

PRACTICE SESSION

Many people discard their old computers when they upgrade. Whenever possible, ask family, friends or neighbours to give their old computers to you and use them to practice bypassing codes and accessing any information still there.

If you do have an old computer handed to you, take a floppy disk apart and cut the actual disk into two or three parts. Then practice reassembling it to access the information (do not try this on good equipment that you may wish to keep, as it can cause irreparable damage).

Surveillance techniques

S urveillance means close observation maintained over a person or group of people. The term used to identify a person or group under surveillance is the target or subject.

In practice, what this actually means is that investigators will carefully watch and monitor a person or a group of people over a given period of time and take a snapshot of their lives, noting and recording the activities in which they are engaged throughout the period of observation. There are several ways of accomplishing this task, which will be explained later. The one overriding factor is to maintain a common-sense approach to the surveillance task.

Surveillance can be of a covert nature, where the observers (usually known as operators) are not seen by the target, or under cover (where the operators are seen but are in disguise, or have taken a false identity and are in close proximity to the target). In broad terms, surveillance comes into three categories:

- Moving, which can be on foot or in vehicles
- Static, which can be in all manner of diverse locations
- A mixture of both

The methods used also fall into three categories, namely:
Loose, where the target is not always in view and can be left for periods of time without continual surveillance.

- Close, which is constant and usually continues for a long period.
- Combined, which allows for periods of surveillance in loose and close modes.

Preparation

There is a mnemonic I was taught when I was training with the Army using all the 'Ps' — Proper Preparation and Planning Prevents Poor Performance. It's not exactly the Army rendition, which, as you might expect, employs a four-letter word to drive the point home. Nevertheless, the sentiment is the same.

Ideally, you should have plenty of time to plan the surveillance properly. In practice though, this isn't always the case, and in the past I have had to put together a surveillance operation in a matter of hours. Experience is an obvious advantage, but experience comes with practice, so I would suggest that you must not be tempted to put together an operation without having had the benefit of several days' preparation, unless you have a lot of surveillance time under your belt.

At the very start, you need to know what the surveillance intelligence will be used for. Ask the person needing the information exactly what they are trying to achieve, then ask yourself if it's achievable from the surveillance point of view. Make sure that you have a good knowledge of law in the area of operations. You should familiarise yourself with the Human Rights Act and local privacy laws prior to your surveillance. All operators should have a basic knowledge of the law, so that they can recognise when a law has been broken and report the fact. When you are satisfied that all the above is in place, you should then plan a reconnaissance of the area of operation. The more time you can spend on the 'recce', the better your chances of success. Obviously, one of the most important aids for you will be a map.

There are many occasions on which you will have to resort to map-and-compass work. In the surveillance context, this skill will enable you to begin planning your operation without exposing yourself too much in the area of operation. A great deal of information can be gleaned from a map, such as the rise and fall of the land. Knowing this may well indicate the best possible direction from which to approach without being seen. Other occasions on which your map-reading and compass skills will come in handy will be when you are describing a particular area of the world in a report to your client or to your team members, or when you are arranging meetings or dispatching them on an investigation to a remote location.

It may be that during your investigation you have followed someone to a remote place, or stumbled across a piece of physical evidence that you need to find again. You may not always be on a well-known highway or in a place that is easily found. In these cases, you will have to know how to take a bearing to pinpoint your exact location with accuracy. On many occasions, I have been involved in serving court proceedings on itinerants, and have had to rely on my map-reading skill to locate them, and then to indicate their exact position on a map that has then been attached to the court papers to show the judge that I attended at the correct place and properly served the papers.

A map is defined as a flat representation of the Earth, or part of it. This representation is one of the basic tools of the investigator. Its proper use should form one of the first skills an investigator masters. Time spent in learning the skill of map work will save a great deal of wasted time in the future. It is the purpose here to introduce you to the very basics of good map reading, and to form a base on which to build and further develop your skill.

Maps show either physical or political features, and their use was first recorded in Babylon in about 2500BC. These primitive maps were little more than large-scale drawings on clay tablets that set out the estates of wealthy merchants. The Babylonians further developed them using astronomical observations to map the then known world. Spies mapping out and planning military campaigns no doubt used these early maps.

By 350BC, the Greeks knew that the Earth was spherical, and by 240BC they could accurately estimate its circumference. This discovery was to lead to Crates of Mallos' first globe 100 years later. In AD160, Greek map-making progressed a stage further when Ptolemy of Alexandria established the network of parallels and meridians as the basis of map construction. He had invented the first 'projection', the method of representing the spherical surface of the Earth on a flat surface.

Ptolemy's methods were adopted and used by mapmakers in the Islamic world, but it was not until the Renaissance that European cartographers constructed their maps along Ptolomaic lines. In 1250, Matthew Paris made his famous traveller's map of England, and by 1300 charts had become more scientific, allowing accurate voyages of exploration. During the sixteenth and seventeenth centuries, instruments for surveying allowed more accurate projections, the most famous being published by the Flemish geographer, Mercator. By 1744, all civilised countries had produced maps covering the majority of the world.

Today's spy-satellite photographs interpreted by computers and modern printing methods make surveying and map construction highly scientific, but the fact remains that the map is nothing more than a flat representation of the Earth, and Mercator's projection is still widely used today.

Two types of map are in everyday use: the topographical and the plan. Both can be used to begin the planning of a surveillance operation. The topographical map shows both physical and man-made features. Topographical map scale (which we shall explain in detail later) varies from 1:10,000 to 1:25,000. For the purpose of planning a surveillance operation, the 1:50,000 can be used to look at a wide area for location and surveillance, while the 1:25,000 gives a good indication of more local features and the shape of the land around the surveillance area. Both can be used to give map references to indicate a precise location.

A plan map depicts built-up areas in such detail that it gives street names and other man-made features. Unlike a topographical map, the plan does not show physical details such as the rise and fall of the land. It is a useful aid to planning, and can indicate parks or open areas of land that may be used to cover a physical approach, and also indicates built-up areas. Most plan maps also show prominent buildings such as police stations, schools and hospitals – all of which will give you a good idea of the area of operations before you commit yourself to a physical 'recce'.

On a map, symbols and colours are used to show features in detail. To understand this, it is best if you think of the cartographer's task. In simple terms, the cartographer starts with a plain sheet of paper. The job then is to portray the 'bird's eye view' of the land in a way in which we can all understand. To do this, the cartographer's first task is to show the relief of the terrain: its shape, rise and fall. This is done with the use of contours — imaginary lines on the ground joined at the same height above sea level. These lines are placed on the map and

PICTURE 19

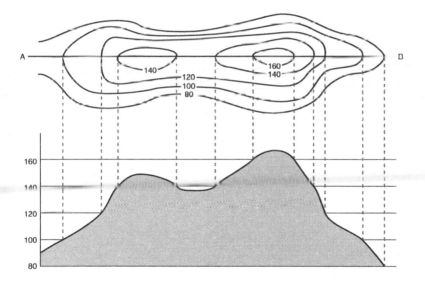

*Maps show relief as a series of lines joined
at the same height known as contours*

show the shape of the land. To express height, these lines are given height values in metres (picture 19).

Contours give a good representation of relief as well as height, and show how steep the feature is. There are other methods of indicating height, the most accurate being a bench mark, shown on the map as △. They are permanent features on the ground, being cut into stone, built into walls or incorporated at the base of concrete pillars known as Trig Points. Trigonometrical heights are the next most accurate, expressed on maps as ⏦. On the ground they are concrete pillars used by surveyors. The least accurate heights are known as 'spot heights', which normally have no visible mark on the ground and are used to show the height of features such as valley bottoms, ridges or hill tops and are shown as a spot with a height value next to it.

Not all maps use these symbols, but the majority do. However, all maps carry a legend that tells you what symbols are being used. Some maps – for example, those used in a world atlas – use coloured tints to show height. This process is called layering. All land above a given height will be shown in a particular tint. Another method is hill shading, which gives a good indication of shape through the use of lighter and darker shades; however, without contours, it gives no indication of height.

As already mentioned, contours start at sea level. However, on occasions it is necessary to show inland features that are below sea level, such as the bottom of quarries. To express depths below sea level, Bathymetric relief is used. This employs contours similar to those above sea level, except that they are usually coloured blue. On modern maps, the measurements are in metres, but on older ones they are given in fathoms (1 fathom = 6 feet). If Bathymetric relief is used on your map, then the datum will be given in the map's margin information.

Once the relief is known, the cartographer's next task is to enter it on to the map sheet using symbols and colours that best describe a particular feature. These symbols can be found in the map's legend or key, and may vary from map to map.

Knowing how the land lies is very important in planning and

executing a surveillance operation. Understanding the relationship between map and ground can only become familiar with constant practice. At first, the difference between your interpretation of the ground taken from the map and the actual ground will dishearten you, but do not despair; as you become more proficient, your interpretation will be more realistic.

During my training, I had to read maps and make models of the ground and building layouts. Since then, I have used this skill to plan several surveillance operations that were particularly difficult or in very sensitive areas of operation.

PICTURE 20

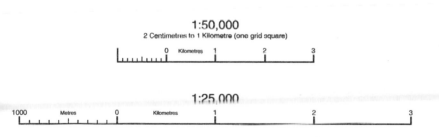

*Maps use linear scale which is used
to measure distance*

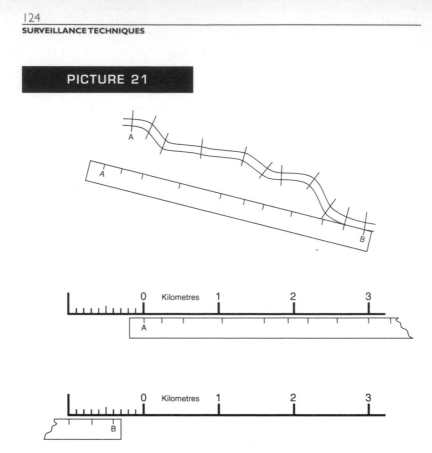

When measuring distance begin at the zero and use the tenths at the end to give an accurate distance

Map scale

Obviously, maps are many times smaller than the areas they cover, yet they are still accurate representations. To maintain this accuracy, the cartographer uses scale. Scale is defined as the relationship between the horizontal distance within two known points measured on the ground and the same two points measured on the map. In practice, it is much simpler than this definition suggests.

Scale is expressed in representative fractions, for example, 1:25,000. This simply means that one centimetre on the map is equal to 25,000 centimetres on the ground. In map-reading, it is important to understand that a change in scale will cause features to be reduced or enlarged proportionately. This means that a feature shown on a 1:50,000 scale map will be a quarter of the size on a 1:100,000 map and an eighth the size on a 1:200,000 scale. Remember that the larger the ratio of the scale, the greater the amount of land that will be represented on the map.

To measure horizontal distance, maps carry a graphic linear scale (picture 20). Note that the zero is set forward from the left of the scale by one full division, which is then subdivided. When measuring distance using this type of scale, you must always remember to start at the zero and end with the tenths (picture 21).

The Grid System

Maps are criss-crossed with a series of lines that form squares known as grid squares. A map's grid system provides a method whereby any point can be defined by a reference to the lines. In addition to this, the grid has three other main functions. It provides a framework within which control points may be computed and plotted, allowing simplification of calculations for bearings and distances. Secondly, it aids the standardisation of maps and the joining together of neighbouring map sheets. And, finally, it provides a framework within which any distortion due to the map's projection can be measured simply and accurately. Only the first two functions concern us here.

As we use lines and numbers to locate certain features on the map, so we use lines and numbers to show the map in relation to its position on the globe. These lines are called meridians and parallels. Meridians indicate longitude and run from pole to pole, and parallels indicate latitude and run around the globe. These lines are numbered in degrees. Zero degrees longitude is at Greenwich, England, and all other longitudinal lines are expressed in degrees, minutes and seconds east or west from there. Zero degrees latitude is at the Equator, and lines of latitude are expressed in degrees north or south from there. This arrangement is known as a graticule, and is mainly used on maps of 1:1,000,000 and smaller. The intersection of graticule lines is expressed on maps using a grid system by a cross symbol, usually in blue. There are two main types of grid system used on maps for land navigation: the Universal Transverse Mercator (UTM) and the British National Grid (BNG).

The UTM is the one most used for military mapping, and covers the whole world except for the polar regions. The BNG covers Great Britain, and is the one used by the Ordnance Survey. Like the UTM, the BNG uses a system based on the Mercator projection. It consists of a series of 100,000-metre squares covering Great Britain. The squares are lettered to assist with location.

Using a map

In a practical situation, the first requirement of a map-reader is to set the map correctly. This can be done in one of two ways, either using a compass (see later) or by visual means. Although in a surveillance planning operation you would be looking at the map before you commit yourself to the ground operation, you still need to know how to orientate a map using the ground. This type of basic map skill will be of use to you in the investigation role to enable you to mark a map properly as part of a report, or to indicate a particular area for intelligence purposes.

To visually set a map is to turn it until the features depicted on the ground correspond with the position of the same features on the ground. Setting the map visually is simple and effective but requires practice. For the sake of explanation, it will be easier if we use this section to underpin the surveillance practice session at the end of the chapter. Using a map of your local area, open the map keeping the majority of the writing the correct way up. In this position the top is northerly, the bottom southerly, left side westerly and right side easterly. Taking the map outside to practice, choose a position that offers you a good outlook of the adjacent area. You need to find a prominent feature on the ground that is easily identifiable on your map, such as a railway bridge, lake, church or some other similar feature. Holding the map in front of you, move it around until the map symbols line up with their respective features on the ground. A common mistake in map reading is for the user to try to read the map with the writing the correct way up – like reading a newspaper. In reality, the map can and should be read from any angle.

Once you are confident in setting your map using prominent features, you should progress to less identifiable ones such as the shape of the land using contours. When using maps in this way, use as many features as possible. It is very easy to mistake one hill for another, especially when you are under pressure.

Finding Direction

From a chosen location, all features lie on a line in a specific direction from that location. Direction is expressed in degrees of a circle, ranging from 0 to 360. There are 16 main directions.

Giving a map reference (six figure)

It may well be the case that you will have to give a map reference to your surveillance team, or as part of a legal process to precisely indicate a position. You may have to work to a map reference to locate your area of operation. In both cases, your knowledge of map reading will be tested. Getting it wrong may well prove costly, both financially and physically.

As explained above, maps are criss-crossed with a series of lines that make up the map's grid. These lines are numbered individually by two-figure numbers shown in the map's margin; these numbers run from east to west and from south to north. To express a particular grid square with reference to its numbers, firstly choose a square and run your finger along an easting (vertical) numbered line to the bottom left corner of the square, then use the same process along the relevant northing (horizontal) numbered line. The two lines should cross at the bottom left corner of your chosen square. It seems complicated, but proves easy when you actually try the process.

Remember that a four-figure map reference will locate a particular grid square. If you wish to find or give a location for a feature within that square, you will need to break that square down into tenths. The simplest way of doing this is to use a Romer, a scale that sets out the tenths within a grid square. Imagine the grid square divided into tenths horizontally and vertically, now take two imaginary lines both horizontally and vertically to intersect your feature. This will give you two single numbers which should be included in your four-figure map reference, and is written as 158:228. You now have a six-figure map reference.

> **NOTE:** the golden rule to remember when giving map references is to give Eastings before Northings; you can easily remember this by the fact that E comes before N in the alphabet.

Using grid letters

I mentioned that the BNG is divided into 100,000 squares and that these are lettered. As individual squares are treated as such, it is feasible that a set of grid numbers may be duplicated on sheets in the same series. Obviously this would prove disastrous if, for example, you put your surveillance operation into full swing but you are using the wrong map sheet. To make map references absolutely clear, you should write the prefixed map sheet letters before the number. You should also record the map serial number so that any follow-up mission can utilise your intelligence correctly.

The compass

A compass is an instrument that shows direction from a fixed line (north:south). The basic design of a compass consists of a magnetic needle mounted on a pivot over a compass card, which allows it to swing freely until it rests pointing to magnetic north.

As early as the first century BC, the Chinese were aware of the principle on which compasses work, but the first sensitive and accurate instrument was Kelvin's dry compass, built in 1876. So reliable was this design that it is still widely used in merchant shipping today.

In 1882, a liquid-filled compass was developed, the liquid acting as a damper to allow the needle to rest much more quickly, thus enabling readings to be taken faster. The compass bowls were filled with distilled water and alcohol. Today's lightweight compass (picture 22) uses the same principle but is filled with oil. As a professional investigator, you should have a compass and know how to use it in conjunction with a map of the area of a surveillance operation.

The majority of map and compass work today is done using the lightweight Sylva type compass, so for this exercise I shall refer to this type only.

Using the compass

As already stated, the compass needle points to magnetic north, which is approximately 1,400 miles south of the North Pole, off the Canadian coast. Because of this 'magnetic variation' from the North Pole, in map and compass work we have to contend with three norths:

TRUE NORTH	The North Pole
GRID NORTH	The North shown by the map's grid system
MAGNETIC NORTH	The area to which a magnetised needle points

There are four main techniques using the compass alone. It enables you to find direction and bearings from your position, follow a direction or bearing accurately, walk in a straight line and return to your starting position.

PICTURE 22

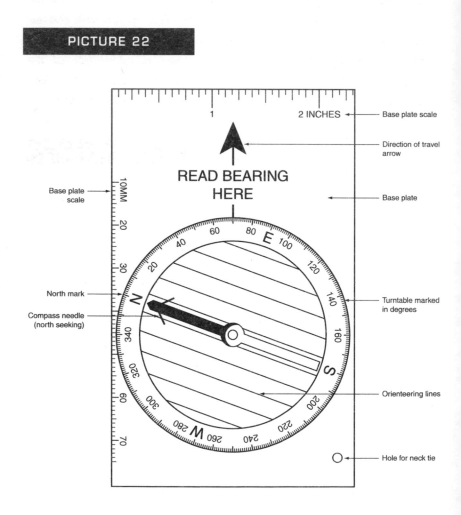

The light weight compass is an invaluable part of the P.I's equipment

Finding bearings (direction)

Using your lightweight compass, find a suitable location such as your local park or playing fields. Choose a feature some distance away, and hold the compass above your waist in the palm of your hand, ensuring that it is level enough to allow the needle to swing freely. Now point the direction-of-travel arrow (picture 24) at the feature you have chosen. Keeping the compass level and in position, swivel the turntable so that the orienteering arrow falls directly below the north side of the magnetic needle. Read off the bearing given at the base of the direction-of-travel arrow. This bearing is the magnetic bearing to your feature.

PICTURE 23

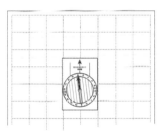

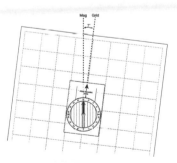

Adjusting the difference between grid and magnetic North is a basic map reading skill

Walking a straight line by compass

As we have already pointed out, as an investigator you could be working in all corners of the world and therefore you may well need to use your navigation skills to effect an escape or to walk on to a specific location for your surveillance operation. One of the skills you need is to be able to walk in a straight line. This seems a simple task, but is not as easy as you might think, especially when you are moving through dense undergrowth or across featureless terrain.

Now choose a bearing and adjust your compass so that the chosen bearing is shown in line with the direction-of-travel arrow. Stand directly behind the compass and place yourself so that the north arrow of the magnetic needle is positioned over the orienteering arrow.

Place a marker at your feet; now simply follow the direction-of-travel arrow, making sure you keep the magnetic needle in position over the orienteering arrow. Count the paces out, then return to your

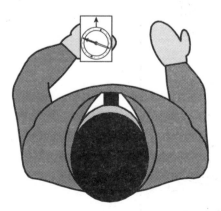

Taking a magnetic bearing to a particular feature will enable you or your colleagues to find it later

starting position by simply adding 180 to your original bearing and follow your 'back bearing' for the same amount of paces to your starting position (picture 25).

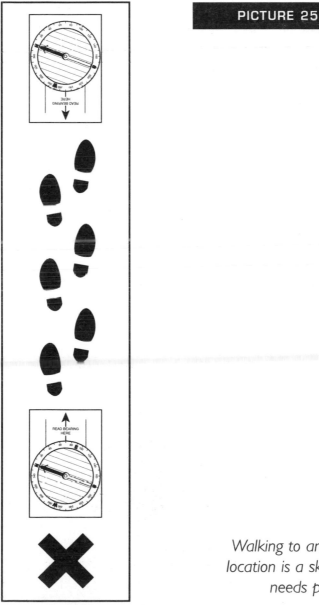

PICTURE 25

Walking to an exact location is a skill that needs practice

Compass errors

Every compass has an individual error, and may point a few degrees away from magnetic north. The needle may not be accurate to the markings on the rose. Every compass should be regularly checked using a known bearing or against another compass of known error. Compass needles are magnetic, and can therefore be attracted by features such as iron, steel, overhead cables, buried pipelines and certain rocks. Even with these errors though, a compass is the most useful navigation aid. A common mistake is to mistrust the compass and rely on your senses, but this is a definite recipe for disaster – always trust your compass.

PICTURE 26

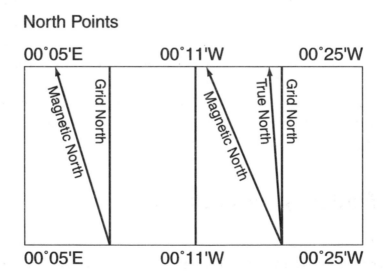

North Points

The different Norths are clearly marked on the map's legend

Map and compass

We have already briefly mentioned the different norths, but what the navigator needs to understand is the 'Grid magnetic variations' – that is, the difference between magnetic north and grid north. Unfortunately, magnetic north moves a little each year. Because of this, maps give the annual change in their margin information (picture 26).

Obviously, it is most important that you check the date of publication of your map and the rate of change before you begin your map-and-compass work.

Setting the map by compass

First, you need to check the magnetic variation on your map from the margin information and adjust your compass. For example, if the magnetic variation were 7° west of grid north, you would have to adjust the compass orienteering arrow by this figure. Then place the compass on the map so that the direction-of-travel arrow lines up with one of the south:north grid lines with the arrow pointing in the direction of north on the map.

Turn the map and compass until the north of the magnetic needle falls over the orienteering arrow (making sure the orienteering arrow remains parallel to the grid lines).

Finding your position

To find your exact position on the map, you need to find two features on the ground that you can identify on your map (such as a hilltop and church). Take a bearing as explained earlier – that is, hold the compass level, point the direction-of-travel arrow at the feature, and adjust the turntable so that the north side of the needle falls over the orienteering arrow. The bearing you have taken is a magnetic one;

PICTURE 27

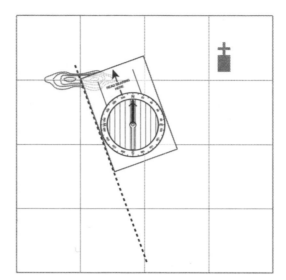

*Finding your exact position will
become easier with practice*

therefore you need to convert this to a grid bearing before continuing.

To convert a magnetic bearing to a grid bearing, subtract the variation. For example, to convert a magnetic bearing of 340°, we take away the variation – in this case 7°, which means that 333° is the correct bearing. The bearing is now adjusted on the compass to correspond with this.

Now lay the edge of your compass on the map so that it crosses your chosen feature. Move the compass around until the orienteering lines on the compass are parallel with the south:north grid lines on your map, and pencil a line in (picture 27). You are now standing somewhere along this line. To determine exactly where, you need to follow the same process using your second feature. The point at which your two lines intersect gives you your position (picture 28).

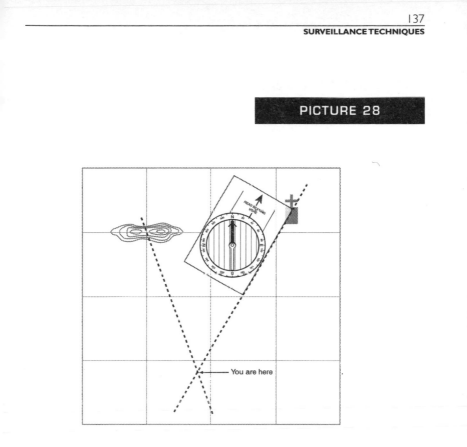

You are here

Where the two lines cross
is your exact position

REMEMBER:

- Choose two easily identifiable features on your map and the ground
- Take a magnetic bearing from both
- Deduct the magnetic variation to give grid bearings
- Pencil in the lines on your map: the point where they cross is where you are

Using map bearings 'on the ground'

Once you have identified your position on the map, you can use your map and compass to move over the ground to a predetermined point – your surveillance area of operations, for example. Simply lay the edge of your compass between the two points and adjust the turntable so that the orienteering lines on the compass lie parallel with the map's grid lines.

Read off the bearing at the base of the direction-of-travel arrow. This is a grid bearing and needs to be converted to a magnetic one before using it to walk by. To transfer the grid bearing, you have to add the magnetic variation. Once you have made this adjustment, hold the compass at waist level, swivel your body until the magnetic needle rests over the arrow, and follow the direction-of-travel arrow to your destination.

Many users get confused when it comes to the magnetic/grid variations. They are simple to remember if you use the following mnemonics:

- **M.U.G.S.** (Magnetic Unto Grid Subtract)
  and
- **G.U.M.A.** (Grid Unto Magnetic Add)

As with all investigation skills, the only way to develop them is to spend time perfecting them. Map-and-compass work is a very important skill, and poor technique will cause you a great many problems.

When you have used your map-reading skills to determine your best approach, you are ready to continue with the surveillance reconnaissance in the area of operations. This may be in a remote area or in an area surrounded by buildings. If you have carried out your map-reading properly, you will know the general layout of the area of operation beforehand, and you can begin to plan the forward observation position properly.

If your surveillance involves you having to observe a building, then you should be looking to find a good static observation position (OP). Getting a plan of the building layout will be of benefit, or, if one isn't available, you should make a sketch plan. Find out where the doors are, and where they lead. Check it out from every angle, use your compass to determine north and think about the sun. Where will it appear on the building, and are you going to be in shade all day? Will the sun be so strong in front of you that it affects your sight? Note the position of the windows – will they reflect the sunlight? Check the positions of outside lights – when it gets dark, will the external lights help or hinder you? A bright light shining from a building gives the building occupants a good advantage; looking out, they are behind the light, and their view will be illuminated. If you are in front of the light then you will be at a disadvantage: the bright light will be difficult for you to look through; your target will be in the dead area behind the light, which is so dark that your eyes will not penetrate it. Likewise, any night-viewing equipment you use will be less effective when it is flooded with direct light.

Find out the interior layout of the building so that if your target moves around you have an idea of what he may be doing in each room. If it is a high-rise building, think about your angle of observation. You will not be able to carry out a positive surveillance operation if you are on the ground floor and your target is on the first, or worse, on the fifteenth. Where possible, you need to have a description of the people who normally use the building, as well as of any vehicles they use. Most of all, you need to have a full description of the target.

When you have decided on the position in which to locate your OP, think about how you are going to get your operators and equipment in and set up without being seen or without arousing suspicion. Once in position, remain alert at all times; this is harder than you may think. A long stint in observation mode takes its toll. Surprisingly, you soon become tired – even though you are not moving around very much. As you start to set up your position, make sure that you cannot be seen. If you are looking through a window, keep well back. Use a dark backdrop, keep your movements to a minimum and avoid causing any reflections from the equipment. Make sure that you cover or, better still, disable any warning or indicator lights on your equipment. On

PICTURE 29

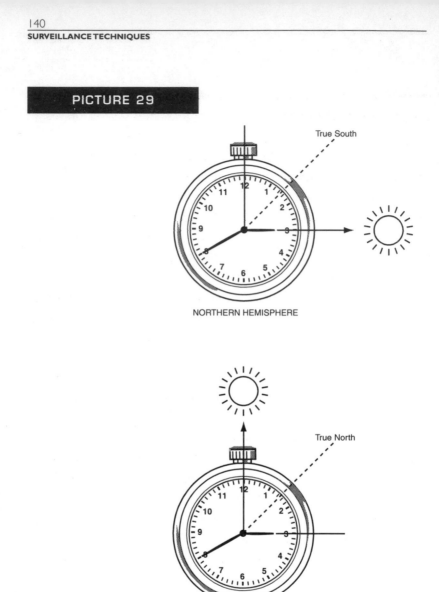

It's not always appropriate to use a compass to determine direction. Using the dial of your watch to determine North/South will be less obvious

more than one occasion, I have seen operators using video equipment, not realising that the 'record' light comes on and can easily be seen from the front.

Smoking is definitely out of the question, as the glow from a cigarette can be seen from a great distance. Not only that, but smoking is an activity and therefore takes your mind away from the job in hand. If you are the observer, then that is the only activity you should be involved in. Take it from me, a lot can happen in a split second, and if you are looking elsewhere at a critical moment, you will miss the action. I have seen this happen so many times – the observer looks away or adjusts his position, and misses the target leaving the premises. For the rest of the day, the team waits patiently and reports that the target never left the premises, only to be told by the client that he had been seen out in the town.

Be sure that your OP is kept in complete darkness and as silent as possible. All communications equipment should be used sparingly and the volume kept low. If your OP is in a static vehicle, be aware that your movements will cause the vehicle to rock. Passers-by may be attracted to this movement and your cover will be blown. Interior courtesy lights should be disabled to prevent them illuminating the observers when the vehicle doors open. If a vehicle is your option, then make sure that it is the type of vehicle that would be used in the particular neighbourhood. Parking the vehicle shouldn't be a problem, but do ensure that other vehicles being parked around it will not obstruct it.

If it is to stay in location for a considerable time, it may be worthwhile telling the local police that it has broken down. On one observation I was involved in, we used a heavy truck parked on a busy road. We removed one of its wheels to demonstrate it had broken down. Although the neighbourhood was a dangerous place and the locals were 'surveillance aware', we managed to stay in location for a considerable time, only coming away after the street children smashed all of the vehicle's windows for a bit of fun, unaware that they were being filmed from the sleeper compartment above.

There are some occasions on which you will have to take up a surveillance role alone. However, this should be avoided if at all possible. In most cases though, you will be part of a surveillance team. When you are working with a team, each member should have a good understanding of the role of the other team members, as well as a good working knowledge of the communications used in the surveillance process.

As well as radio communication, which we have dealt with earlier, the surveillance team needs to be able to communicate non-verbally. Using a pattern of physical signs will enable everyone involved to move and operate as one.

Clearly, if you are working as part of a surveillance team, you will need to communicate with each other as the operation gains pace. Radios are an option, but are not always appropriate, and in fact can be downright dangerous.

On one occasion I can recall, I was carrying out a surveillance operation which was centred on a drug-dealing gang who were using a local authority house. I was placed in the roof space of a house across the street; it was late, and there was no-one around. A police patrol car arrived in the neighbourhood, pulling up outside my location. It was a warm night and they had the car windows open. I could hear their radio conversations – as could the whole district. When they gave control their location, an irate controller came back over the air, his voice bellowing out all over the area: 'Get the hell out of there; there's an undercover team operating down there.' Needless to say, the dealers heard the news and over the next couple of hours they set fire to an adjacent building, believing we were inside.

Non-verbal communication is nothing more than a series of signs which are specific to your team and known by everyone in the immediate operation. You can work out your own pattern of signals if you wish. The advantage of this is that anyone who has prior knowledge of surveillance techniques, such as your target, will not be able to detect the surveillance team.

The signals you use should be absolutely unmistakable. I use a system of hand-to-head movements. As you can see from the diagrams, if the target has turned right, and I am indicating this to the team, I scratch my head on the right side but in a slightly exaggerated way, making sure that my elbow is high and indicating the direction. If the target stops, I stop and look at my watch, again exaggerating the movement with my elbow high. The reason for the high elbow is to properly indicate the direction. This allows you to scratch your head or whatever in the normal course of events without everyone thinking that the target has changed direction. Obviously, you do not

PICTURE 30

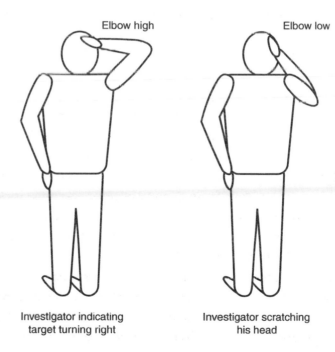

Elbow high Elbow low

Investigator indicating
target turning right

Investigator scratching
his head

*Surveillance operators need a system of simple signs
that look like everyday actions but cannot be misread*

use these signals at every turn or stop.

These signals should only be used as the person with the 'eyeball' indicates the direction to his number two when they change the eyeball, or when a significant event is seen.

Being resourceful and cunning in your surveillance will help you to achieve your objective. There will be many occasions when you will struggle to put the surveillance into place without being compromised. But with ingenuity you will always be able to come up with a solution. On one occasion I had to put together a static close observation on a target who was supposed to be away from work with an injury. The area of operation was highly populated and the target lived in a cul-de-sac.

After some consideration, I hired a truck from a local hire company and turned into the cul-de-sac. One of the team was hiding in the back of the truck. The driver and I were dressed in coveralls, and once we had stopped we got out of the vehicle and posed as refuse collectors with trash bags, and began picking up discarded wrappers and other rubbish. Not only did we film the target working in the garden and cleaning the family car, but the local area also had a good clean.

On other occasions, I have sat with an artist's easel and spent the day drawing and painting, noting the target's movements and visitors. Perhaps one of the most unusual involved my having to wear a diver's dry suit as I lay in a narrow sewer watching a terrorist suspect. When I was extracted, I had a colourful covering of soggy toilet tissues, and none of the team would come near me for quite a while.

There will be times when your surveillance is so close that you are working alongside the target. In these circumstances, you should have at least one other team member either working undercover with you, or close enough to help you if the need arises – a good cover story will be needed. Again, this type of work relies on your ingenuity. It is better if your story is developed from your life, past and present, otherwise you may well run out of life history when you need it most. Using accents that are not your own is extremely dangerous, and can be a dead giveaway.

For example, you may be working undercover in an area such as British troops do in Northern Ireland. You can imagine how surveillance-conscious the local population is there. Anyone who tries to mimic the local accent would soon be picked out – no matter how much training they have. The best way of getting around this is to develop a cover story that is credible and believable; you could say that your family came from Northern Ireland and that you are visiting, for example.

I worked with a gang that was systematically stealing CDs from their employer – a huge European supplier. Because of the way in which the gang recruited its members, I had to have an address in an area that was acceptable to the gang, and which would not be suspicious. Once I had the correct address, I then went along to the recruiting agent for the company and applied for any job with the firm. The only person who knew that I was being put in as a 'plant' was the company director, so I had to get into the job position by the proper route. Once I had gained employment, I worked on a two-shift routine carefully monitoring the workforce until I knew who the gang members were, and eventually became one of them. At the end of the operation, the information I gained led to the arrest of some of the players and the expulsion of others. What was surprising was that the gang was selling the stolen goods in Turkey – not for money, but for motor cars, which were then sold in Russia for US dollars.

As stated before, your choice of clothing is a very important aspect of the surveillance game. In a static surveillance operation, you should wear dark clothing. Black jackets, coats, dark-coloured high-neck sweaters, black gloves and trousers are ideal. Your shoes should also be a dark colour and have a good soft sole with plenty of grip. You can, of course, use a set of black coveralls with a hood and plenty of pockets. This allows you to change quickly from your blacks to your everyday clothes – the problem is that you can also get very hot.

If your OP is in a rural area, then you will probably have to construct a hide and resort to camouflage clothing. In these situations you should have two positions: the first, close to the target, known as the forward observation position (FOP); and a second, safer area further

PICTURE 31

TRAFFIC CENSUS

Being resourceful and cunning will help you to customise your surveillance to suit every situation

away from the target known as the lying-up position (LUP). The LUP allows you to have a relatively safe area for your back-up equipment and for other team members to stay, have their meals and to rest.

When choosing the LUP, consider the route to your FOP. An LUP in ground lower than your FOP makes it safer to move back and forth without being seen. Both the FOP and LUP should be well hidden from prying eyes. Care should be taken in both locations so that anyone in the surrounding area cannot detect you. Choose areas of natural vegetation, and where possible sit well back in the shadow of bushes, or long grass. Keep all movement to an absolute minimum. Have all your equipment close at hand, and make sure that you know exactly where everything is so that you can gather your equipment quickly if you are compromised and have to leave in a hurry. You should be able to put your hand on whatever item of equipment you need to work with even in complete darkness. Everything that you are using in location should be weather-proofed, easy to use and camouflaged.

During lengthy surveillance periods, you should change around with other team members at regular intervals. The way in which you move out of and into location will either help to maintain secrecy or serve to compromise your efforts. Treat the whole thing as the military do – with complete professionalism and stealth. Practice moving around in a slow and deliberate way. In all surveillance operations, be aware of the dangers: constantly review your safety, looking for possible escape routes. Although you are constantly in review, make sure that you do not let your concerns show or stop you from doing your best.

One of the most common problems with the novice investigator is the feeling that your target has seen you, or suspects he is being followed. In practice, this is rarely the case. If you have done everything correctly and with professionalism, then there is little likelihood of your being compromised. The only way of getting over these feelings is experience. Even with experience, the feeling still prevails – it's just that you can cope with it better.

You're now nearly ready to start an actual observation, but before you do so, think carefully about the nature of your target.

If it's a moving target, you will need to know how he usually moves around his environment. A local street map will have to be purchased or made, and possible routes to key points – such as local shops, doctors, bus routes and bars – should be marked out in advance. If he walks, which routes could he take? Does he have a routine? If so, where does he go, and when does he go?

He may own a vehicle. You need to know what that vehicle is and where he usually keeps it. You will need a full description including the colour, registration details and any unusual features such as window stickers or insignia which will help you to identify it quickly when you are picking the target up. The lights should be noted, especially if you are following it through the dark hours. There is nothing worse than following a vehicle through heavy traffic and watching as it merges into a sea of red lights. However, many vehicles do have light faults or distinctive lighting features such as a colour variation, brighter light on one side, or a spent bulb. These distinctive features will help you to pick out your target as he swerves and turns his way to his destination. Most drivers drive in a similar way every time they drive. You need to know whether your target is a slow driver, or a fast driver, or takes risks by weaving in and out of the traffic. All these points will give you an advantage, and the difficult task of mobile surveillance will be made a little easier.

Having thought about all of the above and prepared properly, you will be ready to start the actual observation. Remember to start your recording by opening your surveillance log and ensuring that your electronic recording equipment has the correct day, date and time displayed.

Tailing

As with everything in the investigation field, there is no substitute for experience. However, having good all-round life experience and the ability to think laterally will be a great benefit to you as you gain specific experience in the surveillance field.

Following a target is not an easy task, and is nothing like the way in which you see it done in movies and on TV.

Tailing on foot

In an ideal situation, you should avoid tailing alone; where possible, use a two- or three-man team.

In two-man foot surveillance, operator I has the person being followed in sight all the time (this is known as the 'eyeball'), and should take up a position directly behind the target. Operator 2 should follow operator I either from the rear or, ideally, from the other side of the street. In very busy streets, operator I should be close behind the target, so that the target does not merge into the crowd and disappear from view. Likewise, in crowded streets, the target may make a sudden movement into a shop, the Underground railway system or on to surface public transport. Keeping close will enable the operator to keep in touch with the target at all stages. Operator I should keep the eyeball for as long as he feels comfortable and not compromised. Throughout, operator 2 should be ready to take up the eyeball as soon as operator I indicates this.

One of the best methods of changing eyeball is for operator I to enter a shop, allowing operator 2 to take the eyeball, turning off down a street or carrying on at an intersection when the target turns. In this type of manoeuvre, operator I carries on across the intersection, indicating the direction to operator 2. Ideally, operator 2 then crosses from the other side of the street and takes up the eyeball, and thereby

PICTURE 32

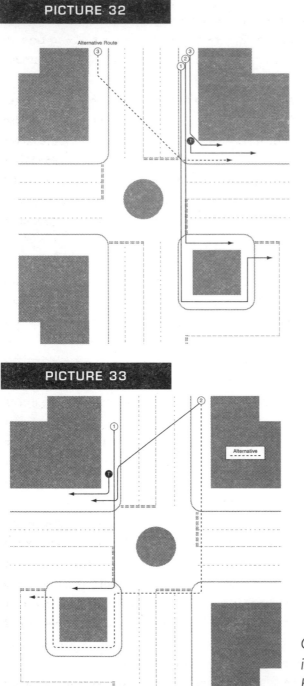

*Three operations
are better than
two in foot tail
operations*

PICTURE 33

*Changing eyeball
is quite easy
but needs practice*

becomes the new operator 1. Once this has been done, the former operator 1, now operator 2, either goes around the block to take up position behind operator 1 or doubles back and takes up the number 2 position.

Throughout the surveillance, keep as close as possible to the target without being so close that your presence arouses his suspicion. Use the reflections in windows as a mirror to the observation. If the target is surveillance-conscious, he may keep looking over his shoulder. Your position should be such that you are out of his line of sight. A useful trick is to keep someone between you and the target so that this person blocks the target's view of you. Obviously, you will sometimes have to risk being seen, especially when you have to move in close such as when the target buys travel tickets or other purchases.

On occasions the target will make telephone calls either from a telephone box or on his mobile. In both cases, you should consider moving in close within hearing range at these times. In practice, this is not as hard as it first appears, as during this type of action the target will be distracted by the conversation. It should be noted though that you should only move in close when it is safe to do so. As the surveillance proceeds, the target may be seen throwing items into a rubbish bin. The operator with the eyeball should indicate this, so that one of the other operators can pick it up and take a look. Often, a target will discard scrap paper or something similar, not realising that they have written down a vital telephone number or details of an illicit meeting, which the investigator can use to further the case.

Although it is possible to get away with a one-man surveillance and successfully operate a two-man team, it is far easier and more productive to use a three-man team. In the three-man foot surveillance, operators 1 and 2 take up the same positions, and operator 3 follows number 2 and takes little notice of operator 1 or the target. Obviously, when the change-over happens, operator 2 takes the eyeball, operator 3 takes the number-2 position and operator 1 takes the rear, relatively safe 3 position.

Tailing on foot necessarily means that you will have to work up close, and consequently you are more likely to be compromised. Having two or more teams of three is an obvious benefit, especially if the surveillance stretches over great distances and many hours.

When the target is surveillance-conscious, he will inevitably try to test his environment and use anti-surveillance tricks to try to pick out any surveillance operators. Walking into a quiet area such as a side street or car park and then turning around and coming back out the same way very quickly can throw an inexperienced operator. In these situations, keep calm and carry on your journey without hesitation. Never look directly at your target. If you've ever been on a crowded underground train, you will recognise what is best described as the 'vacant stare'. No matter how close you stand or sit to another person, your eyes rarely meet – even though you are forced to look at one another, you choose not to engage with them. That is how you should be throughout your close observations. Always keep your eyes on the target, but never gain eye-to-eye contact. Remember, the first thing people look at is the eyes, so make sure that if your target suddenly turns and looks in your direction or, even worse, looks directly at you, your eyes are focused on their torso, not on their face.

On occasions, I have been in the unfortunate position of entering a small room and finding myself face to face with the target. In such a position, it is very important that you act naturally. If in the normal course of events you would be expected to speak, then speak to the target. If he engages with you, then take this up. Do not try to evade him or become invisible – you can't, and any attempt to act in any other way than you would have if you were not in surveillance mode will only serve to confirm any suspicion your target may have had.

In general terms people have an area around them, which is best described as their 'bubble'. Within this bubble they feel relatively secure, but if that bubble is invaded then they feel uneasy. The bubble isn't fixed – it's quite fluid, and moves to different distances when needed. Recognising this will help you with your surveillance. There are three distances.

Intimate distance: This is less than one arm's length. At this distance,

PICTURE 34

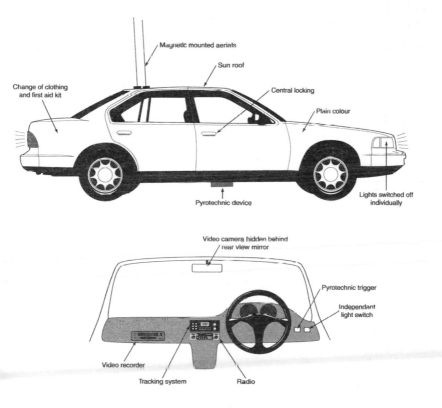

*Most vehicles can be adapted to accommodate
the equipment needed for the P.I.'s work*

either person can choose to touch the other without them having the choice to avoid contact should they wish to do so. Anyone within this distance will be well known to the target, and is usually reserved for very close and special relationships.

Personal distance: More than one arm's distance, but less than two. Any physical contact requires consent. Usually allows private conversations which are not for general release. If for any reason the conversation is broken, the parties will lose eye contact and move away.

Social distance: At least two arms' length. Touching is not possible without moving into an invasive position. This distance is used when parties are not well known to each other.

At all times, be aware of your positioning, and if for any reason you find yourself invading the target's bubble, act appropriately. You should also be aware of the effect your surveillance will have on other people. Be mindful of all those around you who could become suspicious and likely to compromise your operation if you are acting in a way that draws attention to you. Remember, you and the team should blend into the scene. All movements and signals should be smooth and familiar, not jerky and obtrusive.

Tailing with vehicles

I can't emphasise enough the importance of practice in all aspects of the investigator's work, but if there is one area that stands or falls by practice and set drills, it is vehicle surveillance. Not only is a vehicle a dangerous piece of equipment, especially in the hands of an inexperienced person, but it is also the most exposed and easily recognisable part of the investigator's tool kit. An investigator without a vehicle and current driving licence would be like a soccer player without a ball – you can't even start the game.

It naturally follows that your vehicle should be in perfect condition, and clean both inside and out. Each vehicle should carry local and national maps and a comprehensive first-aid kit. Before an operation, ensure that you have checked that all lights and warning systems are operating correctly, and that the vehicle is full with fuel and the engine oil and coolant levels checked. Screens and windows should be clean and screen washers filled. The vehicle should not be conspicuous in its appearance, and should not be out of place in a surveillance operation. In some situations you may have to hire a local vehicle, but for the majority of the time your own vehicle will be acceptable. A dark colour is better than a light one. Luggage racks and other similar accessories such as large aerials, extra lights and fancy registration plates must be avoided. All equipment and paperwork should be out of sight and yet kept in a position to be quickly accessed if needed.

It is also worth having a covert video recorder and camera fitted so that you can record events as they happen. Once again, if you are using this type of equipment, ensure that it is serviceable, and that the day, date and time are properly adjusted.

All communications equipment should be 'pre-op' checked, serviced and fully charged. Mobile telephones should be programmed with the contact number of other team members already displayed, so that they can be operated with a simple push of the Send button. It should all be hands free to allow you to keep both hands on the steering wheel.

Ideally, a surveillance vehicle should have two operators: the driver; and the passenger, who acts as observer and log recorder. Surveillance operators should be dressed in dark clothing and have outdoor clothing to hand. The possible problem with this is that two people in a vehicle do look suspicious, especially if parked up for any length of time. As well as the obvious advantage of the observer role, a passenger can quickly leave the vehicle to follow on foot should the target suddenly go walkabout.

Without doubt, the hardest part of vehicle surveillance is the beginning, known as the pick-up. Obviously the first thing you need to do is to locate the vehicle. This may seem a simple thing to do, but it can in fact be a difficult task. On one occasion, I was part of a two-vehicle surveillance team and located the target vehicle, a red Ford, parked on the driveway of a house. It was dark, and I did a walk past

PICTURE 35

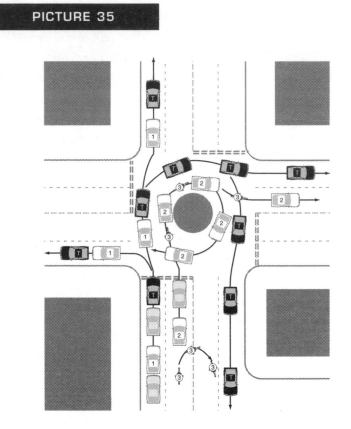

Two cars and a motorcycle is ideal for the vehicle tail

to check the vehicle registration. Having satisfied myself that this was the target, I returned to my car and radioed my colleague, SA 2. He confirmed that he was at the opposite end of the street and also had eyeball on the vehicle.

We sat in these positions for three-and-a-half hours, neither of us making a sound. I could clearly see the driver's side of the vehicle and watched as the driver left the house and started the car. Although I was aware that SA 2 also had eyeball, I broke radio silence with the usual alert: 'Sierra Alpha Two stand by.' The target drove away, heading to the end of the street where SA 2 was positioned. I stayed in my position until the target turned out of sight, and then followed slowly in the knowledge that SA 2 had eyeball. At the junction I could not see the target car and radioed for a sit rep (situation report). SA 2 quickly replied stating he had eyeball and that the target vehicle was still parked on the drive!

At the de-brief it transpired that SA 2 was in the street next to the one I was in and, as you would expect in a residential area, there was another red Ford parked on a driveway, but SA 2 had not checked with a walk-by.

Although it is better to have the eyeball, it is not always necessary or appropriate. For example, your target vehicle could be parked in a garage, or in a location which is so well secured that you would soon be compromised by your presence. In these situations, it is better if you pick up the target as it moves past your location. This type of pick-up will rely on your pre-op planning. Before you can decide on your positioning, look at all the intelligence that you have. You would have already asked your client about the normal habits of the target, and so will have the beginnings of the plan. Take the time to look at local street maps and decide where there will be a bottleneck of the target's movement. At such a place, you can safely park your vehicle and await the target's arrival and effect the pick-up.

Once you have the target in sight, radio that fact to the team and take up your position behind the target. Make sure that you drive smoothly at all times. Erratic, jerky driving will soon be seen through the target's rear-view mirrors, increasing any suspicion he may have had. Likewise, if you are not in the same lane as he is, any weaving in and out to keep up with him will inevitably draw attention to you.

In heavy traffic, you should keep as close to the target as possible without crowding him. Putting a car between you and him is a good way of reducing your exposure, but it often ends with you being stuck at traffic signals. No two-vehicle surveillance is the same, so you will need to adjust your approach to suit the circumstances. When you have eyeball, give a running commentary on your radio to the rest of the team, describing prominent buildings that you are passing and which way

PICTURE 36

*Blending in will be a matter of choosing
the right clothes for the task and disrupting your outline*

you turn at junctions. By doing this, if the team is split then the following members can keep abreast of the tail, even when you are out of sight.

Sooner or later, it will be time for you to hand over the eyeball to your team-mates. Resist the temptation to do this too early, even though you feel you may have been compromised, and even if the target has noticed you. As far as you are concerned, you are simply another road user going about your own business, which just happens to involve you going in the same direction as the target. The change-over should be done as smoothly as possible. Avoid pulling over to allow the following team member to come through – it is better if you turn off the road and allow the change to take place, and then rejoin

Too Much

Too Little

Just Right

Using camouflage cream properly will help you to stay undercover

when the target is out of sight. By waiting like this, the target – if he happens to be suspicious or simply looking through his rear-view mirror – will not see you rejoining the tail.

Although I have dealt with two-car surveillance here, the best possible team is two cars and a motorcycle – all in radio contact throughout. This type of team allows much more flexibility, and can take on long tails stretching for many hours and miles. The weak link – if we can call it that – is, in fact, the motorcycle. A motorcyclist will find it very difficult to sit for long periods of dead time at a pick-up or during a long dormant period. Unlike a car, you do not often see a lone motorcyclist hanging around. Secondly, a motorcycle normally leaves traffic behind in congested areas. It would be unrealistic for a proper motorcyclist to sit in traffic without moving to the front of the queue. Of course, a key strength is its ability to keep up with a fast vehicle and quickly to get into a position behind the target if the other vehicles become hemmed in.

One of the most difficult situations for a surveillance team is when approaching a roundabout. At such an obstacle, the lead car should be very close to the target and in the same lane. The second vehicle should be behind but in the next lane, so that if the target moves across then he is still under surveillance and the lead car does not have to make an irregular move to keep up with him. The motorcycle should be taking up the rear, and be ready to come through if needed or turn around if the target doubles back.

Static surveillance

Although I touched on this subject earlier, it is worth going into it in some detail here, as for the most part static surveillance can move an investigation on very quickly. The amount of information you can gain from a couple of hours is remarkable – add days to it, and you can imagine just how important this can be. Different terrain will present different problems, and it is here that the investigator's ingenuity will always be put to the test.

In rural areas, you will need to adopt a very military approach and select your FOP as a forward observer would do in special forces units. You will need to dress in disruptive pattern clothing, break up your features with camouflage cream and alter your body shape with local foliage. It all seems a little over the top, but in practice you will not want to be seen or be compromised, and so it is therefore a necessary precaution. Dressing in camouflage clothing is no different from selecting clothing that is local to an undercover operation – it's all a matter of blending in, becoming the grey man and completing your objective.

Firstly, you should choose your FOP and LUP as suggested previously. Always remember that you should move into and out of location without being seen or leaving any evidence behind which could compromise your operation.

Some years ago, I was part of a close observation team in a static surveillance operation that involved using an empty apartment adjacent to a drug-dealing gang's headquarters. The operation was spread over several weeks, and involved changing surveillance teams weekly. The change-overs were carried out in the very early hours of the morning to avoid detection. The operation was successfully completed and the final team was left with the clear-up in the apartment.

Having given the evidence to the police, they decided that they would raid the gang's HQ the following week. A second pre-raid surveillance operation was put in place, and one of my three-man teams returned to the empty apartment. On arrival, it was noted that the steel security door had been forced and someone had gained entry. On inspection, it transpired that some of the gang members had broken into the empty building and used it as a squat. Unfortunately, during their occupation they had found two discarded video film wrappers left by the surveillance team.

Having realised that someone had been filming them, the whole gang had packed up and moved to an unknown location. It took us 20 months to locate the gang again and mount another surveillance operation, and a further five weeks before we witnessed sufficient evidence to allow another police raid.

The first part of the operation after choosing the FOP is the team's personal camouflage.

In essence, what you have to achieve is to merge in with your surroundings. The pre-op recce will give you an indication of the terrain in which you will be operating. It would be no use turning up on the op dressed in green if the area was white with snow! Merging in will require you to disrupt your human outline and facial features (pictures 36 and 37). This is done with the use of specially made camouflage cream. You can buy this from most good-quality outdoor, fishing and shooting shops. Brown and green are the best colours for this. There is a single tube that can be purchased and has both colours within it.

The way in which you apply the cream will determine whether or not it will be effective – too much, and you will be picked out by the unusual shape you will be presenting, while with too little you will not have disrupted your facial features enough. However, when you have the balance just right, it is very effective. The best way of applying the cream is either while looking through a mirror or by getting your buddy to put it on for you. The ideal is to dull the shine and smooth out prominent features such as the nose, cheekbones and eye sockets. Having attended to this, you should do the same to your hands and any other areas of exposed flesh.

The next step is to lose your body shape. This is best achieved by wearing a layer of clothing that has disruptive pattern material, such as clothing that is made for use by the military and hunting and fishing enthusiasts. Over this, you should wear a purpose-made camouflage sniper suit as explained earlier (picture 36). These are easily made, usually with brown hessian and by attaching strands of camouflage material and tying on plenty of string laces, so that you can attach local vegetation, allowing you a better opportunity to blend in with the natural surroundings and lose your shape. Practice your approach, as moving while wearing this type of camouflage suit is not easy, and you can get caught on trees and bushes.

You will often move into location in complete darkness. Using night viewing equipment will help, but if you've never used this type of equipment before then you will need to get used to it. In any event, take the time to practice your 'get in' and 'get out'. When the time comes, you will be moving with your surveillance equipment, a pack full of food, water and enough back-up equipment to complete the task. All of this will be of no use if, when you get into location, you can't utilise your specialist equipment.

Generally, as you move around you should avoid giving your position and intention away. Always keep below the skyline, as your silhouette will easily be picked up. Wherever possible, merge into the shadows. People pick out shapes that are familiar or stand out, or movement which is sudden and out of place. Use the natural surroundings to disguise your presence. Remember to sit well back into shrubs and hollows. If your position involves movement across open spaces, try to choose a route that goes around the edges and not directly across the centre. If you have no alternative, then move slowly, keeping low to avoid the silhouette trap. The military use several well-proven methods of movement in hostile territory to avoid detection. You would be well advised to practice these methods regularly in order to master them.

LEOPARD CRAWL

Used to move across low cover with the body at about knee height. Lying flat, move your right leg and left arm, adjust your position and then move your left arm and right leg. All parts of the body should be in contact with the ground throughout. Moving slowly will lessen the noise you make.

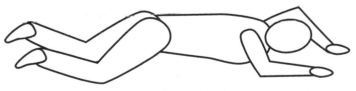

Lying flat

MONKEY RUN

This is a relatively fast-moving style, which allows you to move in cover up to waist height. Once again, the left leg and right hand should move together and vice versa. Using clenched fists will cut down on hand injuries. Fists and lower legs should be the only parts of the body in contact with the ground.

Crawl on hands and knees

GHOST WALK

This is a night walk which requires you to lift your legs very high and then place them down slowly using a sweeping motion to ensure that you are not going to hit wires, fencing or any other obstacle. As the foot nears the ground you should point your toes, placing them down first to ensure a solid platform for the rest of the foot. Your knees should be slightly bent and your arms with outstretched hands and fingers should be moving slowly in large circles to ensure that you are not going to walk into a higher obstacle. There should be no sound. The only part of your body in contact with the ground should be your feet.

Legs lifted high, sweeping slowly to detect wires etc. Knees bent

CAT WALK

Once again, this is a night manoeuvre. It is exactly the same as the monkey crawl, but much slower. Your hands should be feeling the air in front of you and then slowly placed on the ground feeling for any debris that may injure you or make a noise when you put the weight of your body down. Your knee should then be moved up to your hand position and placed in the exact place your hand was in.

Crawl on hands and knees
reaching out to feel for obstacles

KITTEN CRAWL

This method should be used at night in areas where there is no cover at all. It is very tiring, and as such can only be employed for short distances. Lying on your stomach with arms stretched out in front, raise the body so that only your toes and forearms are in contact with the ground. Push forward with the toes so that your body moves forward, and lower yourself to the point where all of your body is in contact with the ground

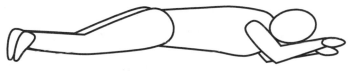

Lift body on toes and elbows
move forward inch by inch

SILENT ROLL

Although I've said that you should avoid skylines, there are occasions on which you will be forced to look over a hill or ridge. Move into position, keeping as low as possible; take a look, and then roll away down the slope.

All movement in this sort of surveillance will inevitably cause some noise, but you should keep it to an absolute minimum. It will help if all of your equipment is secured properly and you tie all straps tightly. At night, people's senses heighten – especially their hearing, which will become acute as their sight deteriorates.

Seeing in the dark

The longer you can keep your night-sight, the better.

The backs of your eyes are made up of millions of sensors that take in light and colour, and are known as rods and cones. Cones are responsible for colour, and have a greater density in the centre of the eye. The rods function better in dim light. As night falls, the rods become more and more sensitive, and adapt your sight to black and white and the grey shades.

Unfortunately, the rods are spread out, so night vision is not as clear as you would like. To allow more of the rods to be activated, the eye's pupil opens wide. Because there is a greater density of cones in the centre of the eye, if you try to focus on an object in the dark then, being colour sensitive, the cones can't cope and your vision is impaired to the point where you can temporarily lose sight of the object. However, if you do not look directly at the object but look slightly to the side, then the rods can pick it up and your vision will be relatively clear. Consequently, to keep a clearer picture, you should continue to avoid looking directly at the object, and keep moving your eyes in a scanning motion so that the rods are kept active and constantly updating your view.

When the eyes are exposed to a sudden flood of light, such as when caught with a flashlight beam or vehicle headlight, the cones are rapidly activated and the pupils quickly reduce. As the light falls back to dark, the pupil opens again but it takes approximately 30 minutes for the rods and cones to settle down and for the pupil to open fully to expose the maximum number of rods, and properly restore your night vision. Where possible, if you know that you will be exposed to short bursts of light, then close one eye. This will enable you to retain some of your night vision.

The undercover operator

Undercover operations

As an undercover operator, your work can be varied and often dangerous. You may be called upon to mount an undercover surveillance operation in a remote area where your only cover will be whatever nature can provide – your skills in camouflage and concealment will be tested to the full. It may be that you have to assume a cover identity and work alongside suspects in a bar, store, warehouse or office, constantly watching their every move, listening to and recording events until there is sufficient evidence to prove theft, fraud, extortion or drug and alcohol misuse. There will be times when you are living and working from dirty disused buildings, cold attics, or assuming the role of a newly housed resident, as you systematically gather evidence of the activities of street gangs, nuisance neighbours and racially motivated crimes and violence. The list is endless, the skills diverse.

Operating equipment in these conditions must be second nature. It will be useless if, when you've successfully moved into location without being compromised, you cannot use your equipment to record the events in all conditions – day and night – with complete silence. One slip of concentration and your cover will be blown, one action out of place will draw attention to you, and one misplaced word can lead to a confrontation and possible exposure. At the very least you will lose your self-esteem, and at worst your life.

In all undercover operations, the trick is to blend in – to become the 'grey man', the person no-one ever notices, an unimportant casual observer, a person who appears to pose no threat. Think about it; are you already the grey man? Or are you the kind of person who enters a room full of people as a 'larger than life' extrovert, immediately in the 'limelight', or perhaps so timid that people are drawn to you out of sympathy?

Next time you enter a room full of strangers, give yourself 10 or 15 minutes and assess the situation. Have you been noticed? Have you blended in without fuss? Whatever the answer, take time to look around: who did you overlook, and why? Analyse them; did you miss them because of the clothes they were wearing, the way in which they were sitting or standing, or was it their lack of eye contact, or their body language? Whatever it was that caused them to blend into the background, you need to recognise it and adopt a similar style.

Clothing is a very important part of the undercover operator's disguise. Before moving into location, study the type and style of the local clothing. Avoid buying new clothing and footwear – nothing stands out more than a bright pair of shoes and shop-pressed jacket, especially when everyone else around you can't afford new clothes. Obtaining the most suitable clothing and footwear is best achieved by visiting local second-hand and charity shops and buying from them. Once you've got your clothing, wear it, work in it and adapt it so that you carry and get to your equipment easily without drawing attention to yourself.

Wherever possible, take the time to visit the areas in which you are going to be working. Look at the people you're going to be mixing with; note their appearance, clothing, the way they walk, talk and act. If your clothes, hairstyle or demeanour don't fit, do something about it; don't be complacent – the locals will be more astute than you think, and they will instinctively know when something is wrong.

When you're employed in undercover surveillance operations that require you to observe, but not to be observed, your planning will have to be absolutely thorough. As explained earlier, carrying out a reconnaissance mission is the best way to begin planning. Remember to consult local maps and guides, which will give you basic information that you can use as your starting point. Without this basic knowledge, you may move into location and find that you are too low to see the target, or there is a physical obstruction blocking your view.

PRACTICE SESSION

Go back over the map reading section until you can orientate your map with and without a compass.

Practice taking bearings and ask your buddy to follow your map and compass references to a given target. Then have your buddy set you a target to find in the same way.

Get your buddy to nominate a friend or family member with a car and practice following them.

Go back over the section on tailing and practice non-verbal signalling, change of eyeball and round about vehicle drill.

Place your buddy on a chair looking into a wood or hedgerow. With camouflage cream and suit move into a location where you can take photographs of your buddy without being seen or heard.

With your buddy in the same position, make a hide and occupy it. Give your buddy binoculars. Once in the hide ask another buddy to place his hand approximately one foot above your head to indicate your exact position. Even with this indication you should still not be able to be seen.

Do the same from a building.

Choose an area and ask your buddy to secretly place objects around that would not normally be seen in the location, such as a telephone on the edge of a pool, or a shoe in a tree etc. Move in to the location with a pair of binoculars and see how many objects you can find.

Practice this at night with your night viewing equipment.

Intelligence

The whole purpose of the work of the investigator is to obtain information and intelligence. The two may at first seem the same, but they are in fact very different.

In essence, information is knowledge that you acquire through your experiences, and is classified as 'primary' or 'soft' information. This may be as a result of your surveillance and enquiries, or acquired by study, through a secondary or hard source, such as information stored in records, photographs, books, registers and databases.

Intelligence is the part or parts of the information that you have collected which is directly relevant to the investigation.

In the intelligence community, there is a cycle that is used to keep everyone focused on the task. This intelligence cycle is made up of five components: direction, collection, collation, analysis and dissemination. Understanding how this simple cycle works will help you to keep your investigations on track.

DIRECTION: First and foremost, everyone involved should be made aware of the reason for the investigation and exactly what it is trying to achieve. If at this stage the needs of the investigation are not clear, intelligence or evidence could be overlooked.

COLLECTION: This is the gathering of information, both primary and secondary. Without proper direction, the information gathered would be flawed and could jeopardise the credibility and positive conclusion of the investigation.

COLLATION: This is where all of the information is examined and compared. It is at this stage that the irrelevant or less important information is sifted out.

The result is the intelligence. This stage is crucial to the investigation. If the person responsible for this does not fully understand the direction and the nature of intelligence, then vital components could be overlooked or discarded.

ANALYSIS: At this stage the intelligence is fully examined to determine its exact relationship to the investigation and its value.

DISSEMINATION: The analysed intelligence can now be distributed to relevant parties so that they can draw on the knowledge, and either bring the investigation to a conclusion or use it to move the investigation on to the next stage.

Having gone through the intelligence cycle and utilised the intelligence, you will probably have a lot of information that you may not need for the investigation in hand. However, this information may well still be important, and may eventually become intelligence either in the current investigation, when the whole thing moves to another dimension, or in some other future investigation.

On one occasion, I was working on a case involving the alleged harassment of a young woman by a local security guard. During the investigation, information was gathered from a number of sources and the intelligence sifted out. Part of the information that was committed to our database was a psychological profile of a stalker. Some months later, I was again working on a similar case that had a stalking element, and reviewed the information on file from the harassment case. Having found the dormant psychological profile, I re-read it and found that much of the profile fitted a particular suspect. The profile entered the intelligence cycle for a second time, but this time it was put forward as part of the overall intelligence and led to the successful investigation and exposure of a stalker.

All the information you gather as an investigator should be kept and recorded, as you never know when it will come in useful. You can do this by keeping the information in indexed file boxes. The problem with keeping information in this way is the incredible amount of room it takes up, and the amount of time you have to spend in locating the correct information.

An easier and more cost-effective way of storing and retrieving information quickly and efficiently is to create your own database. A database is a way of storing information electronically, and you can do this by committing your information to your computer. It will help if you can also scan in photographs and copies of documents so that you can access them in the future. Any photographs you scan in or download from your digital camera need to be carefully interpreted and a short text put with them. There is a skill in properly interpreting photographs – especially those taken from aeroplanes and satellites. The text should explain what the photograph is, when it was taken and by whom, and must point out anything of interest. The idea behind this is that you may not review your picture file for several years, by which time you will have forgotten the reasoning behind the shot. Likewise, the text will help other investigators to understand the context when the photographing investigator is not around to assist.

It is worth pointing out here that if you do keep data or any records, then you should ensure that you conform to the relevant laws, which vary from country to country. In the UK, the Data Protection Act 1998 sets out the criteria. There are eight principles that you should adhere to:

- The information should be fairly and lawfully processed
- It should be processed for limited purposes
- It should be adequate and relevant for its purpose and should not be excessive
- It must be accurate
- It should not be kept longer then is necessary
- It should be processed in accordance with the data subject's human rights
- It should be kept in a secure way
- It should not be transferred to countries outside the EEA without adequate protection

These principles are the basis of the act, although there are some exemptions to registration. It is beyond the scope of this book to fully unpack the act and to analyse its effect. However, I would urge anyone setting up an investigation agency or working as an investigator to seek out the current legislation in the areas of operation.

The database you create will be local to your operation and will be limited by your experience. However, the databases you can access with your computer through the Internet are virtually limitless. The problem is that most investigators do not have the time or experience to look for and find the information they need when they need it. As well as the thousands of databases on the Internet, there are thousands of other sources supplied on CDs and online. All of this information can be useful, but you need to be aware that you could become overloaded with information, and that some of it is likely to be out of date or absolutely wrong.

There is a real need for a dedicated investigator whose job is to constantly work with the investigator's computer. There are few people who have the training to do this job properly and have the knowledge to know what is relevant, current and accurate at the time of the investigation. The job requires a large number of hours' work to learn the different protocols needed to access specific information. Once learnt, the investigator would have to work solely on the computer day after day to keep abreast of the relevant sites and access new ones. The IT investigator also has to have the skill to be able to evaluate the information and know how to organise it so that it can be used as intelligence by the rest of the team or the client.

Tracing missing persons

The IT investigator can often start and conclude an investigation without leaving the office or utilising the assistance of any other investigator. A good example of this is the tracing of missing persons.

Tens of thousands of people world-wide go missing every year for a variety of reasons. Some may be missing because of some criminal act such as murder. Most, though, will be missing because they are running from matrimonial or financial problems, which they feel they cannot overcome or cope with. I am often asked to carry out trace enquiries to ascertain the whereabouts of children who have been taken from their homes, usually by an estranged parent who has not returned the child following agreed contact.

Generally, people who go missing leave a paper trail that can be followed. This trail can be found with the use of databases and online data. For example, telephone directories for the majority of the world can be accessed through the Internet, or you can purchase specific CDs or subscribe to companies that offer you up-to-date details of telephone subscribers for specific areas. Quite often, you can locate an address or person simply by trawling through the directory.

Other databases, CD and online information can easily be accessed. These will include registers of births, marriages and deaths. Birth certificates will give you the date and place of birth, the sex and names of the person as well as the names of the parents and the father's occupation. Marriage licences and certificates will give the date and place of the marriage, and the names and occupations of the parties. Likewise, death certificates will give the date, place and cause of death along with the deceased's date and place of birth and the maiden name of a married woman. In some cases, the name, capacity and address of the informant are also given. Many town and parish registers can be accessed, giving details of burials, marriages and baptisms.

Often a person trying to re-locate will change their name. Registers of changes of names are often kept and stored on databases, as are the details of people who have been naturalised. The information available will be the country of origin and the date of naturalisation. When couples divorce, the particulars of the divorce can be obtained. These will give the grounds for the divorce, and will often give the court's decision on subsidiary matters such as the welfare of the children and financial settlements, which may well include the details of housing and property. The voters' list is a good source of information, and gives details of all the adults living at a particular address. The list can be accessed online either by a direct link to the list holders or through a secondary source such as a credit protection or reference agency.

It is widely accepted that 90% of the information an investigator needs can be found through databases. The problem is finding the right one for the case in hand. A great deal can and should be achieved before the investigation progresses to the street.

There are many ways of gathering evidence from outside sources. I was recently involved in a case where a woman was convinced that her husband, who was a doctor of medicine, was poisoning her sister. The background to the case was that the sister in question had been a very healthy person until shortly after her marriage. The doctor she married had not lived in the area for long and was introduced to her by a mutual friend. Within a matter of weeks they were married. No-one from the doctor's family attended the wedding. Questions were asked, and it transpired that the doctor had not worked for several years as he had been looking after his parents, both of whom had died recently of unexplained illnesses.

Looking at the background and death certificates, it was clear that many of the symptoms the sister had were similar to those of the doctor's parents prior to their deaths. The first thing I did was to get a proper history of the symptoms. Following this I went into a number of databases until I found a forensic scientist whose expertise was in poisons. Having made contact and given the scientist the symptoms, it transpired that these may well have been caused by a particular type of poison. Hair and nail samples were taken and sent to the forensic laboratory for analysis. There was no evidence of poisoning. Even so, the case remains an open one with a watching brief, just in case.

Forensic investigation and analysis can help in many cases, such as with handwriting, documentary examination, finger printing, DNA profiling, blood and substance testing. The list is enormous; however, with the use of databases you can quickly source information and contact experts in a particular field, such as psychological profiling, to assist in your investigations.

The investigation of stalking

If there's one area of investigation in which you have to use most of the investigation skills it is in the investigation, pursuit and eventual exposure of a stalker. The investigation is greatly assisted by the psychological profile of the stalker and the usual target.

The term stalker can be misleading, as it implies that the stalker continually follows his victim. In reality, however, following the victim is only one aspect of his activities. Other behaviour includes verbal threats, which may be delivered in person, or spoken through a closed-door, or from behind a hedge or similar barrier. Letters may be sent, and can range from being threatening and/or obscene in tone to letters of affection; they may also be of a sexually explicit nature, and can often be phrased to invite an answer as a way of gaining information. There may be symbolic gestures – the sending of a wreath or the announcement of the victim's death in a local newspaper. Obviously, following the victim is high on the stalker's priority list. The information gained from this activity can be contained in a dossier and used to intimidate the victim and underline the stalker's intrusion in the victim's life.

A stalker can be involved with his victim for many years, and will use all manner of ploys to gain information about them, and they will quickly locate them if they move areas. Private investigators are often unwittingly used by stalkers to trace the victim. Most people assume that a stalker will be male and the target female. This is not always the case, and many men are the targets of stalkers. It is, however, very often the case that the stalker is of the opposite sex to the victim, although this is not always true.

Stalkers want relationships with people of their choosing – they like to control their victims. They are usually quite inadequate in terms of having and keeping what most people regard as a 'normal' relationship. The stalker forces the relationship on to his victim and gains a sense of feeling better about themselves. This can be because they feel a definite relief of inner tension and experience, an overall feeling of a positive nature. These feelings are reinforced by the ongoing control of the victim, and as a result the stalker proves to be a very persistent offender.

Unlike the majority of people who become the victims of crime, the stalker's victims are usually energetic and successful in their chosen careers. Quite often they are well known celebrities or politicians.

Understanding the needs of the stalker and the type of person usually involved in this type of crime will help you to form your investigation and concentrate your efforts. I find that the best approach to an investigation is first of all to interview the victim in a neutral place – away from the usual places the victim frequents. Because the stalker usually builds a dossier on the day-to-day activities of the victim that is very precise and used as part of the control, the victim often believes that they are being constantly watched and their home, office and telephones are bugged; the neutral venue allows them to feel a little more comfortable. In fact, when I am first contacted, usually by telephone, I quickly cut the telephone call short and ask the victim to contact me from a 'safe' telephone away from home and office. This not only stops the stalker knowing the time and venue of any meeting if bugs are being used, but also signals to your potential client that you are taking the matter seriously.

Many victims think that they are disbelieved and are seen as paranoid by their family, friends and work colleagues. Getting past this quickly and giving the victim a feeling that you do believe their story will help in the interview stage. At the end of the interview, when you have a feel for the investigation, it is worth asking the victim to keep a diary of events, recording what has happened, where, when and whether or not there was a witness to it.

Many victims will already have a diary of past events. It is not unusual to be handed a bundle of recordings running to hundreds of pages at the first meeting. Do not dismiss these, as the client will read into this that you are not interested in their problem. You will not have the time to read these records at the first interview. It is better to ask the client if you can take them with you and read them later. Going through them in detail at a later stage may help you to get a feel for the parties involved.

Once you have the background, you can begin your investigation. It is usually worth having the home and office de-bugged, just in case the stalker has used electronic surveillance. You should then put in place your own electronic surveillance equipment to record telephone calls and conversations between the victim and the stalker that may take place face to face in the office or home. Covert video recording equipment should also be installed in key areas, especially monitoring the outside area of home and office. The recordings should be constant and reviewed daily. By doing this, you may well get sight of the stalker approaching the property or searching through files, workstations or rubbish bins. It is often worth fitting audio and visual recording equipment on the victim, as on many occasions the stalker will approach the victim when they are going about their everyday business.

All events, no matter how small or insignificant they may seem, need to be properly recorded. Eventually, you will be able to pull all of the investigation together and present the police with enough evidence to have the stalker arrested. Police intervention, even just an unofficial interview, is the most effective way of stopping a stalker. Obviously, the more persistent offenders will not stop and often continue stalking their victim during and after a prison sentence. In these cases the victim may consider moving to a different area in an effort to lose the stalker. However, as I've indicated, stalkers can be very persistent and can relocate their victim quickly. The only way to deter them is to continue to investigate them and use the evidence to keep them under lock and key!

It is easy to see how the investigation of stalking can utilise the vast majority of the skills outlined in this book.

Developing techniques

As a way of recapping and underpinning the information contained throughout this book, think about all I have said, and read through the following examples which reflect much of the diverse skills and work you can expect.

Often you will be working as a member of an undercover team. Choosing team members is no easy task, and requires spending time together in team-building challenges before living and working on top of each other in highly stressful and dangerous situations day after day until the task is complete.

In the past I have been with teams in locations that were damp, cold and very dark. Any movement would have compromised the operation. The team members have laid, stood or kneeled in surveillance mode hour after hour, day after day. Hardly a word was spoken, or a movement noticed, performing our body's natural functions into plastic bags and containers which were sealed and kept in our personal holdall ready to be taken with us when the job was finished. No-one would ever have known we were there, and on inspection, no-one would have guessed that four or five operators had ate, slept, emptied their bladders and bowels and gathered evidence for days, and sometimes weeks, never leaving the location.

The same applies in open locations; my teams have operated forward observation positions (FOPs) concealed in bushes, below rock outcrops, in sewers and under garden sheds. To the rear, a second team has set up a lying-up position (LUP), a place which still has its dangers, but away from the main surveillance area. Here the teams can rest, eat, sleep and prepare themselves to relieve the FOP team, each team donned in camouflage cream and clothing, their equipment disguised to mimic the surrounding vegetation. Through rain and snow, summer and winter, these observers have stayed in position relentlessly carrying out the surveillance operation, only leaving to allow the LUP team to take up position, while they move back to eat cold rations and use their plastic bags.

In contrast, within days we have moved into an operational situation where we have been working in a warehouse and infiltrating an organised gang of thieves who have been suspected of the theft of thousands of dollars' worth of CDs, computer games and equipment. By their very nature, these people are suspicious of strangers. It takes time and patience before you are seen as 'one of the gang'. In these operations, you take on a false identity and rely on your back-up team to be ready to come to your aid if you are compromised.

Your new assumed identity should not be too removed from your inner self. Wherever possible, it is better if you retain your name or at least your first name. If this isn't possible, choose a name that has significance to you. By doing this, when the pressure is on you will easily remember it. It would be a mistake to set yourself up as someone who is far removed from the 'real' you. To keep up this pretence becomes more difficult as time goes by. Remember, keep your inner self in the 'new' you. You have views and life experiences – use them to enhance your assumed life, but let them be seen in the proper context, reflecting the type of situation you are working in, with the right emotional balance and appropriate language.

Occasionally, all of these skills come together in one operation. I can recall one such operation when I was a member of a team called in to mount round-the-clock surveillance on a family that was suspected of child abduction. At the initial briefing, lawyers explained the situation and gave us details about the suspects. There were a number of arrest warrants outstanding in respect of several of the suspects, and it was agreed that if we managed to identify any of them during the observations, we would immediately inform the police. We were given photographs of the child and other prominent figures, and each member of the team committed them to memory.

Following the briefing, a reconnaissance team was sent out, which reported that the property had two entrances: one front and one rear. The rear was overlooked by fields and the front by a large, trouble-torn residential estate. A road passed by the front, but was so exposed that anyone parked on it would immediately be viewed with suspicion. The operation plan evolved. Two teams of four operators would undertake surveillance at the property with three pursuit teams of two operators, one on a motorcycle and two in cars parked out of sight. Team A would be dressed in full camouflage and take the rear of the building, team B the front, utilising an empty property on the estate, and team C would take up positions with their cars at opposite ends of the road with the motorcycle positioned to respond quickly in both directions. Besides the surveillance equipment needed for both day and night observations, the communications equipment, and individual rations, team B would also need to take a limited amount of fire-fighting equipment in with them, as we had reports that gangs of locals were firebombing buildings in the area.

With planning and training completed, these teams could operate in the field indefinitely. As it happened, this particular observation lasted seven days with follow-up operations spread over two years.

The diversity of undercover situations tests operators to their limits. To be effective, you have to train and develop skills continually. Turn to the training section for guidance and advice.

Training (general)

Using the example of team surveillance as described above, choose a similar location in the area in which you live. Start by making a simple plan map by firstly extracting relevant information from a local topographical map (as explained in the map and compass section), and then use the information to prepare your basic local plan map. Once you have done this, go to the area undercover, and take in the location and position of prominent buildings, streets, playing areas, etc.

When you have carried out this 'recce', use the knowledge you have gained to make a model of the area of operations. This model can be made out of polystyrene, balsa wood and card. Use toy vehicles to show areas of parking that may obscure views or make a pick-up easier or more difficult. Use the toys to indicate the locations of the team vehicles and the undercover close observation team. Throughout the construction keep in mind that you are going to be using this model to brief a surveillance team that has no prior knowledge of the location. As in the example above, the teams need to know what the objective is, where they are to be placed, the location of the rest of the team, communication and call signs, and the action they should take in an emergency.

Training alone is important for some skills; however, you should have a partner at all stages. This 'buddy' should be prepared to give sound advice and not let personal feelings come between your relationship and your professional training. It would be useless to tell you what you wanted to hear, for by doing so, you would miss the opportunity to sharpen and develop your skills to a higher, more professional level – and you might even be putting yourself at risk.

Being able to take in information and retain it in all situations and conditions is a skill that requires continual honing. During my training, one of the favourite 'games' set out by the training team was to work you, both physically and mentally, until you craved sleep and rest. At the end of a gruelling day, I would fall into a deep and sound sleep, only to be woken in the middle of the night, taken to a cold, dimly lit room, and shown a short feature film lasting around 50 minutes. Tired and exhausted, I would then be taken to another room and questioned about the film in great detail.

This is an extreme illustration, of course, but the benefits have been proven to me time after time. Try it with your buddy. Use a short film to begin with, building to more detailed films. The benefit will be greater, when you're tired and don't want to be bothered with it.

Another simple and effective aid to sharpening your observation skills is 'Kim's Game'. Use your buddy to prepare a tray of assorted objects. Have the tray covered and then presented to you with the cover taken off, view it for one minute, memorise the tray and its objects. Recover and take the tray away. Your buddy should remove one or two objects, wait 30 seconds, and present the tray to you once again. You should be able to tell which items have been removed or replaced. Develop this game to include text. Have your buddy type you a 300-word letter. Read it quickly and hand it back. Your buddy should now give you back a duplicate of the first, but this time with one or two words or phrases missing.

Another good aid to this type of training is a simple game on the streets. Choose a street, and walk along it with your buddy. He should take note of certain features without showing you; for example, how many cars are parked, street signs, prominent features on buildings, etc.; you should take no notes. Out of sight of the street, your buddy then asks you questions about the scene.

The description and recognition of people is a skill that should not be neglected. Sooner or later you will be called upon to act as a witness. You will be expected to describe exactly what you saw and whom you saw. Your description of the person may be the only evidence that links the person to the actual crime.

Having a systematic approach to recognition helps you to focus, even in the most difficult situations. When you are in danger or fearful, you still need to be able to take in and retain information – taking notes isn't always an option.

In very traumatic circumstances, such as hijacking or hostage situations, the professional investigator would be able to blend in, never drawing attention to himself, but always systematically taking in information. There are three reasons for this low-profile approach. Firstly, if you do not draw attention to yourself, when the time comes for the hijacker to choose someone to kill as an illustration of his or her commitment, you're more likely to be overlooked. Secondly, if you don't pose a threat, when the opportunity arises to take control you will have the element of surprise, and thirdly, if you're fortunate to be released early, your descriptions and superior observations will be invaluable to the authorities.

From now on, get into the habit of looking at people as a professional investigator. Start with the overall impression. How tall, what age, male or female, tall or short, fat or thin? It helps if you can put the overall person into a look-alike category, such as a famous person or one of your friends. When you've taken this first appraisal, go into detail, starting at the head, noting the colour of hair, length and style; the eyes: size, shape colour, etc. Work slowly down the body, taking particular note of any distinguishing marks such as a scar or tattoo. Clothing can be changed, but nevertheless take note of what they're wearing, especially their watch, bracelet, necklace or rings.

Although people can easily change their appearance, they rarely manage to alter their mannerisms. The way they move, and particular habits, are very important aspects of their character.

Team building

As an investigator, you will have to carry out most of your day-to-day work alone. As you have seen throughout the book, there will be times when you will have to function as a member of a team, either as team leader or a team member. You may be fortunate enough to have a surveillance team that operates full time. A long-term team does benefit from team-building activities outside the normal team objectives. Sometimes you will have to put a specific team together to perform a particular task. These specific teams can be highly motivated and very task centred.

Not too long ago, I was asked to investigate a case involving a high-profile businessman who was supposed to be attending a meeting in Nairobi, Africa, but in fact he did not attend the meeting. The following investigation revealed that he had gone to Beirut, Lebanon. People who knew him stated that they were concerned because although he had family there, it was unlike him to miss the meeting and not to let them know where he was. Their concern was that he was being held there against his will. The continuing investigation indicated that this was likely, although it seemed that his forced stay was more to do with the pressure of his family than unauthorised detention. Nevertheless it was agreed that I would travel to Beirut undercover as a world trader, find him and then ask whether or not he needed help to get him out. Along with me would be the extraction team, who was likewise undercover with a variety of false identities, just in case he decided he wanted to leave. The team and line of communication would stretch from the UK to the Lebanon, with several escape routes built in to secure the team and the target.

In this kind of situation, you need to be able to fully trust members without any doubt about their individual commitment and team responsibility. Putting an effective team together is not an easy task, but the hard work is well worth the end result.

To be effective, a team has to have three core components:

- Accomplishable goals, either formal or informal
- Maintaining the team by ensuring that the team members' individual needs are met and that the team develops effective ways of working together
- That there is an ongoing development and changes are made to improve the effectiveness of the team
- To maintain and develop these core components, the team members must be encouraged to assume particular roles that allow their individual skills to be used effectively and to develop those skills to meet the team objectives

The skills needed broadly fall into 16 key areas:

- A complete understanding of the team's goals
- Individuals understanding the needs of the other team members
- The ability to motivate the other team members
- Being able to communicate ideas to others
- Being able to communicate personal feelings to others
- Having the ability to participate in the team's activities
- All the members need to be able to take the lead role if needed

- The ability to understand that the team has to work closely together and to be able to work towards achieving the team's cohesion
- The team members must be allowed to use their skills to explore issues, discuss and contribute to the planning and decision-making process
- Each member should be able to choose and recognise the priorities to work towards the team goals
- They should have the ability to use their own power, influence, expertise, knowledge and skill to good effect, and be able to assist the rest of the team members to utilise these for the benefit of the team objective
- Conflict within the team can be a very destructive influence. Team members need to be able to deal with any conflict in a positive way, and to recognise that minority opinions can be useful and should not be overlooked
- Team members have to have the ability to cope under extreme pressure and danger, and enable other team members to cope by presenting a positive and confident outlook throughout
- They have to be able to develop and maintain dependence and trust in each other
- Team members must recognise the importance of working together to realise the team objective
- They must be able to problem-solve by inventive thinking and implementation

Once a team can develop the above and work together, there is a great deal that can be achieved. Long and protracted surveillance tasks can be undertaken and produce astounding results.

The best way of selecting and proving a team is to have a series of what can best be described as 'shakedown camps'. These camps should be arranged in such a way that prospective team members have to live and work together. They should include hard and hazardous tasks and challenges for the participants to tackle as a team. During this selection process, you should be looking for members who fulfil and contribute to the list above, and can work as group members and motivate the group without any detriment to the other members in the overall team.

The leader role has a slightly different bias. The leader should be able to perform as any other team member and fulfil the criteria in the same way. The team leader also needs to develop the following components:

- **TACTICS:** To take on the overall planning of the best ways to achieve the objective
- **EQUIPMENT:** To have an overall knowledge of the technical details of equipment and methods to achieve the team task
- **PHYSICAL EXERCISE:** To maintain a level of fitness that allows the leader to lead the team in strenuous and lengthy tasks
- **KNOWLEDGE OF THE LAW:** To have a good overall knowledge of the law in general, and to be able to access and acquire relevant legislation and law in the area of operations. He should also be able to carry out a risk analysis in line with health and safety legislation
- **METHODS OF INSTRUCTION:** The ability to impart knowledge to the team by quality teaching and presentation skills, and to be able to develop a relevant and interesting training programme that can be utilised as and when the work schedule permits

Joining a recognised organisation

Joining a recognised organisation can greatly increase your awareness of current issues in the investigation industry, as well as keeping you up to date with current legislation and changes in the law that affect your day-to-day work. As well as these very important aspects of your life as an investigator, joining a recognised organisation will give you the opportunity of meeting like-minded individuals whom you can call upon to give advice and guidance that will usually be based on a sound working knowledge of the industry.

Most organisations will have a code of ethics that you should consider and adhere to. The following is the code as used by the Association of British Investigators (ABI):

- To perform all professional duties in accordance with the highest moral principles, and never to be guilty of conduct which will bring reproach upon the profession of the private investigator and the Association of British Investigators.
- To verify the credentials of clients and that they have lawful and moral reasons to instruct an investigator.
- To respect the privacy of clients and their lawful confidence.
- To ensure that services are adequately secure to protect privacy and to guard against inadvertent disclosure of private information.
- To ensure that all employees and other persons paid to assist an investigation adhere to this code of ethics and to accept responsibility therefor.
- To conduct all investigations within the bounds of legal, moral and professional ethics.
- To respect the best interests of our clients by maintaining the high standard of proficiency and reporting to our clients all the facts ascertained:

whether they be advantageous or detrimental: and that nothing be withheld from the clients save by the dictates of law.
- To work together with all members of our association towards the achievement of the highest professional objectives of the association, and to observe the precepts of truth, accuracy and prudence.

There is no overarching organisation in the United States that handles PI Work. Because licensing varies by region, organisations tend to also be by state or region of the country. Or, they deal with member directories, trade magazines and advertising, etc.

Licensing

Be careful. Licensing can be mandatory. Most states and some cities require licensing to call yourself or practice private investigation within their boundaries. To practice private investigation without a license can lead to fines, prosecution or even jail time. Getting a license may require working in a field that requires investigative research for a certain number of years, passing a class and exam and paying a fee and apprenticing to a PI. Others locals require nothing. Remember also that because the rules and requirements to work as a Private Investigator can vary by city and state, a PI cannot necessarily follow leads or work in other states unless that state has reciprocity agreements with the state in which he is licensed. Because the requirements are so varied, we don't have the space to list all of the information here. The rules for licensing, regional laws or contact addresses for all states and are readily available over the internet.

Useful Addresses

THE ASSOCIATION
OF BRITISH INVESTIGATORS
ABI House
10 Bonner Hill Road
Kingston-upon-Thames
Surrey KT1 3EP

THE INSTITUTE OF
PROFESSIONAL INVESTIGATORS
Suite 353 Glenfield Park Business
Centre
Blakewater Road
Blackburn BB1 5QH

THE WORLD ASSOCIATION
OF DETECTIVES
PO Box 333
Brough HU15 1XL

COUNCIL OF INTERNATIONAL
INVESTIGATORS INC.
2150 N.107th, Suite 205
Seattle, WA 98133-9009
USA

SELECT ASSOCIATES
INTERNATIONAL INVESTIGATIONS
PO Box 10
Herrington
Stoke-on-Trent STG 0LY

DATA PROTECTION REGISTER
Wycliffe House, Water Lane
Wilmslow
Cheshire SK9 5AF

WORLD INVESTIGATORS
NETWORK INC.
PO Box 6656
Baltimore, MD 21219
USA

Individual State Private Investigation Associations and/or Licensing Information

http://www.crimetime.com/licensing.htm

NATIONAL ASSOCIATION OF INVESTIGATIVE SPECIALISTS
P O Box 33244, Austin, Texas, 78764 Phone 512-719-3595 Fax 512-719-3594 Email: RThomas007@aol.com

THE NATIONAL ASSOCIATION OF LEGAL INVESTIGATORS (NALI)
6109 Meadowwood, Grand Blanc, MI 48439
Telephone (800) 266-6254
Fax (810) 694-7109
www.nalionline.orginfo@nalionline.org

COUNCIL OF INTERNATIONAL INVESTIGATORS INC.
2150 N. 107th, Suite 205 Seattle, WA 98133-9009

Tools of the Trade and State Links

PI Mallhttp;//www.pimall.com 703.780.9033